30-Minute COOKBOOK FOR BEGINNERS

30-Minute COOKBOOK FOR BEGINNERS

100+ RECIPES FOR THE TIME-PRESSED COOK

COLLEEN KENNEDY

ROCKRIDGE
PRESS

Interior & Cover Designer: Patricia Fabricant
Art Producer: Maura Boland
Editor: Brian Sweeting
Production Editor: Matt Burnett

Photography ©2019 Iain Bagwell;
©Hélène Dujardin, p xii
Author photo courtesy of ©Kara Hartwell Raudenbush

ISBN: Print 978-1-64611-699-7 | eBook 978-1-64611-700-0

R0

TO JOHN, CONNOR,
AND SAMANTHA,
MY FAVORITE PEOPLE
TO COOK WITH
AND FOR.

Contents

Introduction

I have enjoyed cooking for as long as I can remember. I'm not sure what excites me most—thinking of something I want to eat, then walking into the kitchen and making it happen; the sense of satisfaction I get when I make something that becomes a new family favorite; or the feeling I get when the food I cook makes others happy. If I had to choose, I'd say what I enjoy most about cooking and baking is when it makes others feel happy, satisfied, excited, and—my favorite—loved.

Whenever one of my kids says how good something is as they eat it, my reply is always "MWL!" MWL means "made with love." When you go into the kitchen to make a meal for yourself or for others to enjoy, my advice is to be happy and add a little love. It tastes better!

For those of you who have not yet ventured into the kitchen or think you can't cook, all you need is the desire to cook; the rest will unfold. Find a recipe you want to make, read it through, gather your ingredients, get organized, and have at it. It's really that simple. And the more you cook, the better you will become at it.

This book shows you how to prep your kitchen, gives you organization and shopping tips, and points out some great tools and ingredients every home cook should have to make their time in the kitchen as easy as possible. It also covers all sorts of basics to set you up for success.

All the recipes in this book can be made in 30 minutes or less, and some have just five ingredients or fewer. I hope you will be pleasantly surprised by the dishes you create and that some of my favorite recipes, such as the 10-Minute Salsa (page 52), Zucchini Cakes (page 83), Lemon Pepper Pork Chops (page 133), and my absolute favorite, Crab Cakes (page 100), become some of your signature dishes, the ones people in your life rave about.

Is everything you make going to be perfect? Nope! Trust me, I have kitchen fails every so often—everyone does. But unless you push yourself to move from the mantra of "I can't cook" to actually exploring cooking, you will never come to see just how easy it can be. If you can read, you can cook.

I hope that as you cook your way through this book, you learn a few tips and tricks, become a more confident home cook, and try a few recipes that are new to you. But most of all, I want you to taste and adjust the recipes to your liking and find where you can put your own spin on things. If you have kids, let them help! Getting them into the kitchen while they are young and letting them help—and sometimes allowing them to take the lead—will not only make them better eaters but also help them grow up to become confident home cooks themselves.

1

How to Prep Your 30-Minute Kitchen

A lot of us *think* we can't cook. I am here to say, "Yes, you can!" All you need is a bit of strategic organization, some forethought, a healthy dose of enthusiasm, and practice. In no time, you'll be dazzling your family and friends with your tasty creations.

In this chapter, I'll set you up for success by showing you how to prepare your kitchen for efficient, 30-minute cooking, which you'll put to good use in the recipes in later chapters. I'll give you tips and tricks on grocery shopping, food storage, and time-saving equipment. In short, I'll give you the confidence you need to start cooking. You've got this!

Why Faster Is Better

As much as we might like to spend half the day cooking elaborate meals or spend hours at the table lingering over dessert and coffee, that fantasy rarely becomes reality. The truth is that between school, work, activities, and the demands of modern life, our reality is usually all about getting food on the table as efficiently as possible.

However, that efficiency doesn't mean the food you put on the table can't be as delicious as an indulgent holiday feast. At home, many of us approach making meals as a chore—something we need to check off our to-do list. But planning out even a few meals in advance, shopping smarter, and learning a handful of techniques will save you time in the kitchen (and save you money, too). Learning to cook—and learning to cook efficiently—will help you avoid relying on other time-saving options such as fast food and heavily processed, often unsatisfying microwavable meals. With a little practice, you'll soon start thinking of cooking not as a burden, but as an enjoyable activity. And the less time you spend preparing your meals, the more time you can spend enjoying them with family, friends, and loved ones.

Shop Smarter, Not Harder

The first step in becoming an efficient and successful home cook is making a plan before you go grocery shopping. Too often we buy ingredients we don't need or that we think we *might* use. When those foods are perishable (e.g., meats, fruits, or vegetables) they may linger in the refrigerator and eventually end up in the trash.

Here are some tips for efficient grocery shopping:

Decide which meals you're going to make for the week ahead and draw up a corresponding list. This is a surefire way to minimize food ending up in the trash. You'll also be able to spot ingredients for one recipe that can be used in another, and where you can repurpose leftovers (for example, one night's rotisserie chicken is another day's chicken salad).

Shop your pantry first (see page 4). You may already have in your pantry or refrigerator all or most of the ingredients you need to make a recipe.

Only buy produce you know you will use that week. If something interesting catches your eye, take a picture and work it into your next shopping trip. Curb the impulse buys and reduce waste by knowing how you will use any ingredient before you buy it.

Frozen produce is better than you might think. Stocking up on frozen essentials gives you easy access to integral ingredients without you having to worry about freshness, thus increasing the variety of recipes you can make on any given day. Plus, many vegetables and fruits are flash-frozen at their peak, meaning they are actually fresher than those found in the produce section.

Know your budget. Use coupons and check the store flyers for sales. Often, grocery stores have extra savings on weekends. Check prices; in many cases, you can get a larger size of something for almost the same price. Try store brands for some products, especially if you buy organic pantry items; many stores have own-brand organic lines.

Avoid shopping when hungry. Trust me, everything looks *really* good when you're starving. Stay on task and only buy the items you need.

PACKAGED VS. PROCESSED

Most foods in any grocery store have been processed in *some* way prior to packaging. They may have been cut, cooked, frozen, canned, or roasted for your convenience. However, these products (e.g., sliced fruits, bagged vegetables, canned beans and fish, roasted nuts, and more) retain their inherent vitamins and minerals and can dramatically speed up kitchen prep time.

Processed foods, on the other hand, typically contain unhealthy fats, lots of sugar, and unnatural chemicals, additives, and preservatives. These foods include sweetened cereals, flavored potato chips, margarine, frozen meals and pizzas, many sauces and dressings, flavored crackers, packaged cookies, and more. Although it may not be realistic for you to avoid processed foods completely, this book is designed to help you stop relying on the kind of processed foods that may have sped up your meal preparation in the past.

When in doubt, read the ingredient labels. If you spot high fructose corn syrup, sodium nitrate, propyl, potassium bromate, or monosodium glutamate on the labels, it means those foods are typically high in trans fats and sugar and you would do well to avoid them.

THE GROCERY SHOPPING (CHECK)LIST

Don't forget to make a list before heading to the grocery store. An easy trick is to keep a running list on your phone, because your phone is always with you. Another thing to remember is reusable shopping bags. Taking your own bags not only cuts down on waste, but they're also much sturdier than plastic shopping bags, allowing you to hold much more in them and keep your groceries organized.

When you get to the store, first check for any deals, which are often displayed on a board or on flyers near the entrance. Some stores have two- or four-day sales that are often very good. Next, start shopping in the meat or seafood section and make sure what you're looking for is available. Then hit the produce section to make sure you can get the vegetables or fruits you need for your recipes. If something is out of stock, you may have to pivot and swap out a protein or re-plan your meal. And remember: If you need help finding something, don't be afraid to ask.

Trust me when I say that going to the store with a plan and a list is the best way to shop. It will save you time and money and reduce food waste.

How to Stock Your 30-Minute Kitchen

Having the right ingredients on hand at all times will enable you to make your favorite recipes efficiently and also improvise dishes on the fly. In the following sections, you'll find lists of essential items to keep in your pantry, refrigerator, and freezer. Some are time-savers, and others are flavor-builders. Over time, you'll discover which ones you like (and need) the most.

THE PANTRY

Here are a handful of staples you'll want to keep in your pantry.

Baking soda and baking powder. Both are leavening agents, which means they help baked goods rise. (As an added bonus, baking soda can clean a crusty pan better than anything.)

Bread crumbs. These are great for making meatloaf, meatballs, chicken, and more.

Canned tomatoes. Canned tomatoes are fantastic for making quick home-made pasta sauce, soups, stews, chili, and salsa.

Flour. Flour is necessary for both baking and thickening sauces or dips.

Garlic and onions. Both are used as a foundation to build flavor in soups, stews, vegetable dishes, and sauces.

Honey. Honey is a wonderful sweetener for tea, sauces, marinades, and baked goods.

Oil. Olive, grapeseed, and avocado oil are all good choices. All three are fantastic for making dressings and marinades as well as for sautéing. Avoid partially hydrogenated oils and palm oil.

Pasta. Choose a variety of shapes and sizes for pasta dishes, soups, and salads.

Rice. Choose a variety for sides, salads, soups, stews, bowls, and more.

Seasonings. Staples include kosher and sea salt, black pepper, cayenne pepper, red pepper flakes, paprika, cinnamon, Italian seasoning, chili powder, garlic powder, and onion salt.

Tortillas. Tortillas are great for breakfast burritos, wraps, quick pizzas, and tortilla chips.

FOOD STORAGE 101

Most canned goods will stay good for at least six months, so it's a good idea to check their expiration dates at least twice a year. Store the items with the latest expiration dates toward the back of your pantry area. Once you open a canned item, store what remains in an airtight container in the refrigerator for maximum freshness and shelf life. Dry items can be kept in an airtight container in your pantry.

It's important to store oils, honey, potatoes, garlic, and shallots in a cool, dark place—a bin in your pantry would be ideal. Check them weekly for spoilage. If potatoes smell moldy, toss them; if garlic has green shoots or brown spots, throw it away.

Lastly, whole spices tend to stay potent for up to two years, while ground spices should be replaced every six to eight months. To test them for freshness, sniff them. They should smell strongly of their spice. If they smell musty or don't smell of much at all, toss them.

THE REFRIGERATOR

Here are some items to keep in your refrigerator that you won't want to do without.

Bacon. Can you ever *not* have bacon in your refrigerator? Besides using bacon for breakfast, you can use it as a topping on salads, sandwiches, and even some desserts.

Butter. You can never be without butter. It's the key to many baked goods, lends a wonderful flavor to sautéed vegetables, and tastes fantastic on a slice of toast.

Cheese. Hard cheeses (e.g., Parmesan and Cheddar), soft cheeses (e.g., Brie and mozzarella), and crumbled cheeses (e.g., feta) have many uses in salads, dips, and pastas.

Eggs. You already know eggs are great for breakfast, but they're also a key component of many recipes, from meatballs to fried rice to salad dressings.

Lemons and limes. Fresh lemon or lime juice brightens up a dish and is great for making marinades and salad dressings.

Mayonnaise. Mayo is used for everything from sandwiches to dips, sauces, crab cakes, and more. Plus, it's the secret to a killer grilled cheese!

Meat. If possible, buy protein fresh and keep it in the refrigerator. If you don't end up using it in time, you can always freeze it (see page 7).

Scallions. These are an underrated garnish for soups, biscuits, savory quick breads, marinades, and more.

Soy sauce. This staple in Asian cooking is used in a number of recipes in this book. I recommend buying low-sodium soy sauce.

Sriracha. A wildly popular hot sauce that's often used as a condiment, you can use Sriracha in marinades and sauces.

Worcestershire sauce. This pungent ingredient is a fantastic addition to marinades and sauces.

EXPIRATION DATES 101

Food expiration dates exist for a reason: to keep us safe.

Most foods feature two expiration dates: the "sell by" date and the "use by" date. The "sell by" is a suggestion to consumers to purchase a product before that date. Products will typically be more visually appealing and fresher before the sell by date; however, the USDA notes that you can, in fact, still use products for a short time after the sell by date. Just use common sense, as well as your senses of both smell and taste.

The "use by" date should be taken more seriously, especially with refrigerated products such as meat, poultry, dairy, and eggs. Typically, you can eat something a day or two after the "use by" date, but you generally want to avoid cutting it that close. Again, use your sense of smell here. If an item smells funky, don't eat it. And when in doubt, throw it out!

THE FREEZER

Having these items on hand in your freezer may save you a trip to the grocery store and make cooking impromptu meals and snacks easier.

Berries and fruit. Fruit that you either freeze yourself or purchase frozen is great to have on hand for smoothies and baked goods; think strawberries, blueberries, mixed berries, and mango.

Meats. In my opinion, chicken holds up best frozen. You can also freeze beef, pork, and other varieties of meat if you need to. When meat is frozen, ice crystals form, resulting in a loss of natural juices when the meat thaws. The key to successfully freezing meat is getting as much air out of the package as possible and using freezer bags. Less or no air will prevent discoloration as well as freezer burn. Poultry can keep in the freezer for up to six months. Meat and seafood are good for three months. For optimum freshness, store the protein in its original package inside a freezer bag, and remember, the fewer air pockets, the better.

Shrimp. If you enjoy shrimp, stock up when it's on sale. Shrimp thaw quickly and are wonderful for grilling, sautéing, adding to salads, or simply eating as shrimp cocktail.

Vegetables. Frozen vegetables are great for side dishes, soups, stews, and dips (I'm looking at you, chopped spinach). Consider broccoli, corn, edamame, peas, and carrots, which are the vegetables that hold up to freezing best.

DEFROSTING 101

There is a right way and a wrong way to defrost food. First things first: Never defrost anything in the microwave. No matter how careful you are, it will start to cook, which causes two problems: One, your food will not be as fresh, and two, bacteria will begin to form. If you must use a microwave to defrost any meat, poultry, or seafood, you should cook it as soon as it's defrosted.

The safest and easiest way to defrost a piece of meat or poultry is to place it on a plate, either in its original packaging or in a freezer bag, and leave it in the refrigerator for 24 hours. If it's a larger bone-in piece, it may take up to 48 hours to thaw completely. If you're in a rush, keep the original packaging intact, place it in an airtight baggie, and submerge it in cold water, changing the water every 30 minutes so it continues to thaw. Smaller proteins may defrost in an hour or less, whereas a 3- to 4-pound piece may take up to three hours.

To defrost vegetables or fruit, remove them from any packaging, place in a colander, and run cool water over them until they're thawed—typically 30 minutes. To save water, you can always place them in the refrigerator in their original packaging on a plate the day before, or in the morning on the day you choose to use them.

Essential Equipment for Your 30-Minute Kitchen

In addition to standard baking sheets, cutting boards, mixing bowls, measuring cups (for dry and wet ingredients), measuring spoons, a few good pots and pans, and a vegetable peeler, the following tools are essential to efficient cooking.

Blender. This will save you time making thick soups, smoothies, condiments, and more.

Box grater. This will help you quickly and easily shred cheese and vegetables such as zucchini, potatoes, onions, and even tomatoes.

Chef's knife. A good quality chef's knife, such as a Wüsthof, Cutco, or Henckels, will last forever if you care for it. You will use it every day you cook, and it will help you cut ingredients safely and more efficiently.

Digital instant-read thermometer. This helps you avoid overcooking and undercooking meat.

Kitchen shears. With a pair of shears, you can save a bunch of time when snipping herbs, scallions, sausages, and more.

Manual chopper. If you don't have a food processor, a manual chopper will chop onions, carrots and garlic in seconds.

Metal spatulas. Get a small, rectangular, 3-inch spatula for good control when moving cookies and eggs, and a square 3-by-3-inch spatula for lifting lasagna and steaks.

Stand mixer. If you plan on baking often, a stand mixer, which is an electric mixer with a bowl and a whisk attachment, is a necessity. Use it for cookies, cakes, and for making the best whipped cream in under a minute. If you bake often, I recommend getting an extra bowl for it.

Whisk. You'll want one of these for making sauces, dressings, eggs, and batters.

TIME-SAVING TOOLS

While you don't *need* some of the following pieces of equipment, they do make working in the kitchen much easier—and much faster.

Food processor. This is hands-down my most used and most efficient small appliance. Chop or mince vegetables in seconds, make a paste, salad dressing, sauce, or pesto in under a minute, and so much more.

Hand chopper. My favorite, favorite, favorite time-saving kitchen tool by far. If you don't have a food processor or don't feel like chopping by hand, whip out the hand chopper. The one made by Pampered Chef is the best (in my opinion), although OXO and KitchenAid make them as well.

Ice cream scoop. Besides scooping ice cream, a scoop is handy for easily measuring and placing consistently sized portions of cookie and biscuit dough on baking sheets.

Immersion blender. This tool is relatively inexpensive and amazing for making sauces and soups smooth. Just stick it right into your pot or bowl, turn it on, and bam—smooth as silk!

Microplane. This makes zesting citrus for garnishes and more a breeze.

Potato masher. This will make mashing potatoes and other ingredients, such as bananas for banana bread, much, much easier.

Rice cooker. If you eat a lot of rice, an inexpensive rice cooker (under $25) is worth its weight in gold. Set it and forget it!

Toaster oven. When you don't want to wait for the oven to preheat and you just have something small to bake or reheat, a toaster oven does the job.

Tongs. Locking tongs with silicone/nylon tips are phenomenal. They make quick work of turning meats and veggies when cooking.

HOW TO CLEAN WHILE YOU'RE COOKING

Take it from me: Knowing you don't have a big cleanup waiting for you after preparing an elaborate dinner is a truly great feeling. In fact, it makes the subsequent meal all the more enjoyable.

First off, you'll want to keep your workspace clear of dirty dishes, tools, and ingredients you no longer need while you're cooking. Put dirty cutting boards, utensils, and dishes directly in the dishwasher or sink after you've finished using them. Return any refrigerated ingredients or dry goods right back where they came from as soon as you're finished with them. Wipe down the work surfaces often to keep them clean and to prevent cross-contamination. Use a garbage bowl for food scraps, and slide the trashcan over to where you're working for easy disposal of waste.

The Importance of Mise en Place

The French term *mise en place* (pronounced meez-ahn-plass) was the first thing I taught my kids when they began seriously helping me in the kitchen, around the age of five. Mise en place sounds fancy, but it's not complicated. It translates to "everything in its place." In the context of the kitchen, that means having the ingredients and equipment for a recipe ready to go *before* you actually begin to cook or bake. For some people, that means every ingredient is measured out, all the vegetables are chopped up, and all the meat is trimmed. For others, it means all the ingredients are set out with measuring spoons and cups at the ready. However intense you are about your own mise en place, the point of doing it is to avoid having to stop preparing a dish halfway through making it in order to search for an ingredient—or worse, finding out you don't have it.

Taking the time to set up your mise en place makes cooking a whole lot easier. The more efficient and organized you are, the more likely you are to achieve the desired results and the less stressed you will be during the process. Cooking is all about planning, organization, and follow-through. Think of yourself as the project manager. If you were cooking a steak, for example, and you heated the pan, added the oil, and then realized you had to go find the steak seasoning, the oil might begin to burn—and because you want to do justice to the meat (and what you paid for it), you would have to wait for the pan to cool down, clean it, and start again. Not the best use of your time, right?

Here are some hard-and-fast mise en place rules to follow before you start cooking:

1. Make sure you have ample space cleared and cleaned for your prep area.

2. Gather all the ingredients.

3. Set out the necessary tools, bowls, cutting boards, and cookware.

4. Chop and measure.

5. Clean up as you go.

2

Time-Saving Techniques

Part of any home cook's kitchen confidence stems from mastering the basics: knife skills, safety, and essential cooking techniques, from pan frying to broiling. In this chapter, we'll cover all that and more, including reading recipes, time-saving kitchen hacks, and methods to maximize your microwave.

But First, Let's Talk Kitchen Safety

The most common kitchen injuries are burns, cuts, and falls. To stay safe, stay focused on the task at hand and follow these tips:

☞ Put a damp dish towel under the cutting board to prevent it slipping around while you slice, dice, and chop.

☞ Never look away from what you are doing when chopping, mincing, or cutting.

☞ Always be aware when you have a knife in your hand, especially if you have younger children in your home. Don't suddenly turn around with the knife in your hand. When a knife is not in use, make sure it is out of the reach of curious little hands.

☞ Always use oven mitts and pot holders. As a reminder that a pan is hot, slide an oven mitt onto the handle after you remove the pan from the oven.

☞ If you spill something on the floor, wipe it up right away.

BACTERIA

Food safety when cooking is important, especially when working with poultry, meats, and seafood. Following these tips will help keep you and those you cook for safe and your hands and surface areas free of bacteria.

1. **Wash your hands.** First and foremost, wash your hands every single time you enter the kitchen to work with food. Wash them again after handling any type of raw meat, poultry, seafood, raw eggs, or eggshells (or anything those foods may have touched). Wash them once more after you finish cooking. Use warm soapy water and wash for 20 seconds or more, paying special attention to the underside of your fingernails as well as your wrists.

2. **Thoroughly clean all surfaces.** Wash cutting boards, dishes, utensils, and countertops with hot, soapy water, especially after they've held raw meat, poultry, seafood, or eggs.

3. **Sterilize the sink.** Your sink is one of the germiest spots in your kitchen. To keep microorganisms to a minimum, you should disinfect your sink at minimum once a week as well as after handling raw meat, poultry, seafood,

or eggs, or their juices. To clean the sink, use hot soapy water and a clean sponge and clean the perimeter of the sink, followed by the sink itself. For a deeper clean, use hot water and vinegar or hot water and a small amount of bleach.

4. **Avoid cross-contamination.** Cross-contamination is the unintentional transfer of microorganisms and/or bacteria from one area or surface to another. It's a good idea to keep one cutting board for working with raw meats and a separate cutting board for everything else. Also, you can't effectively clean something with a dirty sponge. Clean your sponge at least weekly by submerging it in undiluted vinegar, which will kill close to 100 percent of germs. Replace the sponge every two to three weeks.

5. **Never wash poultry or meat.** No matter what you read, just don't do it. This is the leading cause of cross-contamination. Meat and poultry are produced and packaged safely by professionals to be ready to cook. The heat during cooking will kill any other harmful bacteria. The following table provides the internal temperatures meat and poultry should reach before they're safe to eat.

RARE BEEF (COOL RED CENTER)	125ºF
MEDIUM-RARE BEEF (WARM RED CENTER)	135ºF
MEDIUM BEEF (SLIGHTLY PINK CENTER)	150ºF
WELL-DONE BEEF (NO PINK)	160ºF
MEDIUM-RARE PORK	145ºF, plus a 3-minute rest
MEDIUM PORK	150ºF
WELL-DONE PORK	160ºF
GROUND BEEF AND PORK	160ºF
CHICKEN OR TURKEY	165ºF
FISH	140ºF

The USDA recommends steaks and roasts be cooked to 145°F (medium) and then rested for at least 3 minutes. To ensure food safety, ground beef should be cooked to a minimum of 160°F (well done). Be sure to check the temperature with a thermometer, as the color of the meat alone is not a foolproof indicator.

BURNS

Accidental burns and fires are a concern in any kitchen. To avoid burns and kitchen fires, always pay attention to what you are doing and what is going on around you. Be careful of your hands when around anything hot, keep an eye on the stove whenever it's on, and follow these rules:

1. Make sure you have a working smoke detector and, ideally, a kitchen fire extinguisher.

2. Don't leave food cooking on the stove unattended. If you need to leave the kitchen, turn off the heat until you return.

3. Keep flammable items, such as wooden spoons, food packaging, paper and dish towels, and oven mitts, away from the heat source.

4. Fire needs oxygen to survive, so if a fire breaks out in the oven, do not open the oven door. Turn the oven off and move away; the fire will go out on its own.

5. If a fire breaks out in a pot, carefully place a metal lid on the pot to smother the flames and prevent any oxygen fueling the fire. If a fire starts on the stovetop itself, either scatter baking soda onto the fire to smother it or use a fire extinguisher. *Do not use water.* Most kitchen fires are a result of oil, and water will react with oil particles, causing the fire to spread.

6. If the fire cannot be put out and seems to be spreading, go outside and call the fire department.

To avoid burns, always slide a pot holder onto the handle of a pan as soon as you remove it from the oven or when working with pots and pans that don't have heat-safe handles. If you have kids, keep hot cookware away from the edges of the stove or countertop where little hands could reach them. In the event of a burn or injury that breaks the skin, seek medical attention. For minor burns, cool the burn by submerging it in cold water or placing a cold compress on the burn. If you have it, apply burn cream or petroleum jelly to soothe the burn. Keep the area clean by covering it with a bandage.

BLADES

Cuts can happen any time you are working with a sharp knife or sharp kitchen tool. Heck, you can even get a nasty injury from a potato peeler or from washing a blender. The key to staying safe in the kitchen is to always pay attention to what you are doing and to what those around you are doing. Sure, you may be chatting with someone as you prep and cook, but keep your eyes on your hands and on what you are doing when working with a knife or other sharp kitchen tool. Here are a few hard-and-fast rules to avoid cutting yourself in the kitchen:

1. Use the "claw" method (see page 18) for the fingers holding the item to be cut.

2. Cut away from yourself, not toward yourself.

3. Don't try to cut anything that can roll away from you. When cutting fruits or vegetables, first cut them down the middle and place the flat side down.

4. Always use a cutting board. Never cut anything up in the air or in the palm of your hand. Place a damp kitchen towel under the cutting board to make sure it doesn't move.

5. Always wear close-toed shoes when working in the kitchen in case something hot spills or something sharp falls.

6. Keep your knives sharp (see page 18). Dull knives require more effort to use and can cause slippage. Sharper is safer.

Knife Skills

When you hold and move your knife properly, it does the work for you just as if it's an extension of your arm. The knife you will use most when cooking is a chef's knife, which is the kitchen "workhorse." Once you are comfortable using it, your chef's knife will become your most prized kitchen accessory.

Here's how to hold a chef's knife: Pick up the knife in your dominant hand. Look at where the blade meets the handle. Take your thumb and your pointer finger and "pinch" the metal where it meets the handle. Wrap your other fingers and hand around the handle. Relax your grip and let the knife do the work.

Always have the fingers of your opposite hand (the one holding in place whatever you're about to cut) in the shape of a "claw" or an angry letter "C" with the tips of your fingers pointing down onto the food and your fingernails acting as a shield.

Contrary to what you may think, a dull knife blade is actually more dangerous to use than a sharp blade. Here's why: A dull blade requires more pressure to cut, increasing the chance that the knife will slip. Purchase an inexpensive sharpening stone to keep your knives sharp; you can also pay to have your knives sharpened locally. American-made Cutco Knives offer a Forever Guarantee—simply send in your knives, and they'll sharpen them and send them back.

TYPES OF CUTS

Texture, doneness, taste, and presentation are all factors to consider when deciding which cut to use. Here are some of the most common cuts:

Chop. To cut a vegetable or fruit into similarly sized, bite-size (or smaller) pieces, about the size of a dime. To chop, you first cut the ingredient into larger chunks and then go over them with your knife. For example, chopping ingredients for soups or chopping chicken or tuna for a cold salad.

Dice. To cut something into small, similarly sized cubes to ensure even cooking. Dicing does not have to result in perfect cubes, just pieces of the same size. Recipes may call for a small dice, a medium dice, or a large dice. A small dice is considered to be ⅛ inch wide, while a large dice is typically ¾ inch wide. To dice, start by halving the ingredient, then slicing it into strips. Finally, cut the strips into small or large dice. For example, dicing a mango for salsa, dicing carrots or potatoes for pot pie, or dicing vegetables for fried rice.

Halve. To slice a vegetable or fruit down the middle, resulting in two evenly sized pieces. For example, halving a peach for grilling, halving a head of lettuce for shredding, or halving a lemon for squeezing.

Mince. This means to cut food into very tiny pieces. After you chop a vegetable, go over it again and again with the knife, cutting it smaller with each pass until it's no bigger than the head of a matchstick. Minced food typically dissolves by the time the dish is complete. For example, mincing garlic, ginger, and herbs for marinades, stir-fries, and curries.

Slice. To cut vegetables, fruits, meats, or breads into thin, similarly sized rounds or slices. First, you would halve a fruit or vegetable. Next, you would slice it into thin strips. For example, slicing vegetables for a salad, slicing raw chicken or steak for a stir-fry, or slicing bread for a sandwich.

Snip. Instead of a knife, use kitchen scissors or herb cutters to snip herbs into small pieces with ease and with less bruising than a knife. You can also use kitchen shears or scissors to snip long sausage links into bite-size chunks.

HOW TO PREP AND CUT VEGETABLES

Remember mise en place? Having your vegetables cut and portioned out according to your recipe instructions before you begin cooking is a great example of mise en place. You can section the ingredients out on a cutting board or in prep bowls so they'll be at hand when you need them. Here are some preparation instructions for frequently used vegetables:

Garlic. To cut garlic, first remove the number of cloves needed from the garlic bulb, then remove the paper from the clove(s). Slice the clove into 3 or 4 slices then turn your cutting board and slice those slices into tiny cubes. To mince, run over those cubes back and forth with the knife a few times until the pieces are the size of a matchstick head.

Onions. To chop an onion quickly, halve the onion and peel off the papery skin. Place one half flat-side down on the cutting board and hold it firmly in place with your fingertips in a "claw" position (see page 18). Cut off and discard the stem end of the onion. Leave the root end intact to help the onion stay together as you cut. Next, make lengthwise cuts into the onion, from root end to stem end. Then make crosswise cuts, making sure to hold the onion firmly with your fingers "clawed."

Tomatoes. To chop a tomato, first cut off the stem end, then halve the tomato lengthwise. Place one half flat-side down on the cutting board and carefully slide the knife down left to right (or right to left depending on which hand you use) lengthwise, making two long halves of the tomato. Keep both halves in place with your fingertips in a "claw" position (see page 18) and cut the halves into strips. Turn your cutting board and then cut those strips into cubes. Because tomatoes are so delicate, a serrated knife works best here; you really want to saw through the tomato gently, as opposed to pressing down too hard and potentially squishing it.

Peppers. To chop any variety of pepper quickly, first slice off the top and bottom of the pepper. Cut the pepper in half, remove and discard the seeds and stems, then slice the pepper into even strips. Cut those strips into small "squares" by slicing across a few strips at a time.

Quick Cooking Methods

There are numerous cooking methods, but let's start with some of the basics. These are great to have under your belt in order to get meals on the table quickly and efficiently. These methods are the most commonly used in the recipes in this book.

PAN COOKING

When you want a hot meal on the table in a hurry, stovetop cooking is the way to go, using either a frying pan, griddle, sauté pan, or pot to get the job done. The most common techniques are pan frying, sautéing, searing, and stir-frying. Let's explore each below.

Pan Frying

Pan frying is frying food in just enough oil or fat to glaze the pan, which results in a crispy brown exterior and tender interior of the fried food. Start by heating the pan on a burner set to medium-high heat. When it's hot, pour in a little (usually a tablespoon or so) grapeseed oil, olive oil, or other chosen fat, followed by the protein or vegetables. You should hear a sizzle as you place the ingredients in the pan. Start cooking over medium-high heat to get the exterior of the food crispy, then reduce the heat to finish cooking through without burning or drying out the food. It's important to not crowd the ingredients in the pan. Leave plenty of space between pieces of food, otherwise the food tends to steam and remain pale in color rather than get browned.

Sautéing

Sautéing typically refers to cooking smaller pieces of food, such as chopped vegetables and meat, over medium heat until they are cooked through. Keep in mind that the more similar in size the ingredients are cut, the more evenly they will cook. If the pieces are too large or too thick, there is a risk of burning the outside before the inside is cooked.

   This quick and easy technique begins with heating the pan for a couple of minutes on medium heat, then adding some fat, typically olive oil or butter. Once the fat just begins to shimmer, carefully add the protein or vegetables, stirring or turning the pieces occasionally. Because sautéing is a quick process, always have your food cut, prepped, and ready to go before you begin cooking. Skillet pans and sauté pans work best for this method.

SMOKE POINTS

When you pan cook most foods, you typically need fat in the form of oil or butter. These fats conduct heat, add flavor, and prevent the outside of the food drying out. Similar to how water reaches a boiling point at 212°F, fats reach what is called a "smoke point," generally at much higher temperatures, up to 500°F.

Different oils have different smoke points. If you don't pay attention to the smoke point, the fat will begin to break down, giving the food an undesirable taste. Usually, you should place meat in the pan once you see the oil shimmer or little ripples form. If you wait longer, the oil will begin to smoke and could ruin your food or, even scarier, the oil could catch fire. The higher a fat's smoke point, the higher temperature it can withstand and the more you can do with it.

EXTRA-VIRGIN OLIVE OIL	325–375°F
BUTTER	350°F
COCONUT OIL	350°F
SESAME OIL	350°F–410°F
AVOCADO OIL	375°F–400°F
GRAPESEED OIL	390°F
CANOLA OIL	400°F
VEGETABLE OIL	400–450°F
PEANUT OIL	450°F
REFINED OR LIGHT OLIVE OIL	465°F
SAFFLOWER OIL	500°F

Searing

Searing, or cooking food in a pan over high heat, gives meat, fish, and poultry an attractive brown exterior, deepening both the flavor and the texture.

Cast iron or stainless steel pans work best for searing; however, you can also use a heavy nonstick pan. Just as when pan frying, use a large enough pan so that your food isn't crowded.

First, heat the pan over high heat. While it heats, pat the protein dry with a paper towel. Even if you marinated the protein previously, pat it dry before it hits the pan. Add a little oil (usually about 1 tablespoon), and as soon as the oil begins to shimmer and ripple, carefully add the protein to the pan.

Searing some foods, such as the Seared Scallops on page 103 and the Skillet Steak and Potatoes on page 138, will cook them completely. Other foods, for example the Blackened Pork Tenderloin on page 128, must finish cooking in the oven. When searing food that will subsequently go into the oven or a pot, hold it with tongs and carefully sear all sides to give it a good color.

Stir-Frying

Stir-frying is a technique of cooking meat and/or vegetables in a small amount of oil over very high heat. When stir-frying, the food is typically cooked in just a few minutes, so it's critical to have all the ingredients chopped, measured, and within reach of the stove before you begin cooking.

A wok works best for stir frying; this traditional, round-bottomed Chinese skillet has a bowl-like shape that allows you to quickly move the ingredients around (or, you know, "stir-fry" them). That said, if you don't have a wok, a large stainless steel or cast iron pan with deep sides will also work. Fresh ingredients are best for stir-frying. Never use frozen meat; it won't cook evenly and it's difficult to tell when it's properly cooked.

The Beauty of Aromatics

Aromatics are vegetables such as garlic, celery, carrots, and ginger, and herbs such as thyme, saffron, sage, and bay leaves that are cooked in oil and impart their flavors to the oil and the dish. Cooking aromatics in oil encourages their flavors and aromas to release, creating a deep flavor foundation for soups, stews, sauces, meat fillings, and more. Plus, they make your kitchen smell delicious!

To get going, heat the wok or pan over very high heat. Add the oil, then toss in well-seasoned meat or fish, followed by some aromatics (see the sidebar on page 23), and stir it frequently. Finish everything off with a splash or two of soy sauce, rice vinegar, or the sauce of your choice, and voilà—your stir-fry is ready!

BOILING

Boiling is a quick cooking method typically associated with pasta, hardboiled eggs, and some green vegetables—broccoli, for example. To boil water, fill a pot about halfway with water and place it over high heat. When it starts bubbling consistently, it is boiling. The goal is to keep the heat under the pot at a level that keeps the water in constant motion, with bubbles repeatedly rising to the surface. The "rolling boil" keeps the cooking food in motion with minimal assistance needed from the cook.

Gentle Boil vs. Rolling Boil

A gentle boil, also known as a simmer, is accomplished by bringing a liquid (typically water, stock, or a sauce) to a boil over high heat, then reducing the heat to low, or by gradually raising the temperature until the water just begins to boil. A gentle boil is best when making sauces, for example, because the slow simmering builds flavor and thickens the sauce.

A rolling boil is achieved by heating liquid over high heat until large bubbles repeatedly come to the surface. It is typically used for quick-cooking items such as pasta or hardboiled eggs, and green veggies such as broccoli. It can also be used to tenderize vegetables (quickly give crisp vegetables, e.g., carrots, a crisp-tender texture) or to blanch vegetables (partially cook them).

Steaming

Steaming refers to cooking with the heat of the steam produced by water at a rolling boil. Vegetables retain much more flavor and nutrients when steamed as opposed to being submerged in boiling water. To steam, bring a pot partially filled with water to a rolling boil and insert a steamer basket (or even a small metal colander) filled with the food you want to cook, and cover the pot. The water should not touch the food. Steaming is a quick and easy way to cook broccoli, green beans, corn, edamame, pot stickers, clams, and mussels.

BROILING

The broiler in your oven is basically an upside-down grill. It's used when you want to quickly cook something at a very high heat. The broiler can be used for melting cheese on lasagna or nachos, cooking a thin piece of fish or meat, or finishing a steak or roast chicken. You can of course burn the heck out of food quickly if you aren't paying attention, so when you are broiling, be vigilant. Some people without a grill choose to broil their steaks (carefully flipping the steak midway). Using the broiler successfully takes practice, but it can be a great, efficient tool. For a good introduction to the broiler, try the Grapefruit Brûlée (page 33).

Some broilers are positioned in the top part of the oven. If using an oven broiler, you typically want to move the oven rack to 4 to 5 inches below the broiler element, to lessen the chance of burning the food. Check on the food often, making sure it's cooking evenly and not burning. Broiling is always a quick cook.

You may instead have a broiler located in a drawer below your oven. In this case, try to position the rack in the drawer 4 inches or so away from the broiler (you don't have as much flexibility with a drawer unit as you do with a standard oven).

When ready to broil, turn the broiler on and allow it to heat up for 4 to 5 minutes, just as you would with a gas grill. Next, slide the prepared food on a baking sheet under the broiler and cook briefly, typically 7 to 8 minutes, depending on what you're cooking and the thickness of the food.

MAXIMIZING THE MICROWAVE

Most kitchens contain a microwave, but almost no one takes full advantage of it, usually only using it to reheat leftovers, melt butter, and cook the occasional potato (although potatoes are so much better when cooked in the oven).

However, the microwave is useful in other ways, too—cooking bacon, for example. You can use it to soften sweet potatoes or butternut squash to expedite their cooking or baking time. Another use of the microwave is for melting chocolate chips for chocolate-covered pretzels, fruits, and nuts.

There are some rules when using a microwave:

☞ Never turn a microwave on (set to cook) if it's empty. You will literally destroy the unit and possibly start a fire.

☞ Always use microwave-safe cookware. If you do not see the words "microwave safe" on a dish, do not use it in your microwave.

☞ Never put metal of any kind in the microwave, and that includes aluminum foil. It will catch on fire.

☞ Always cover any food you are reheating with an inverted plate, if possible, or a paper towel, to prevent splatter. (Do not use plastic wrap; there's no need to possibly melt plastic into your food.)

When you do use your microwave to quickly reheat leftovers, reheat the food in short 60- to 90-second bursts. That way you prevent it overcooking and drying out. Adding a small amount of water (½ to 1 tablespoon) to the food when reheating vegetables, rice, grains, or pasta prevents it from drying out and allows some steam to add moisture.

THE MOST COMMON COOKING HACKS

There are an infinite number of shortcuts chefs take to save time preparing their food. The following hacks and tips are some of my favorites, and will make you a better, more efficient home cook.

☛ Revive whole or half loaves of bread that are a few days old by quickly running them under water and then placing them directly on the rack in a preheated 380°F oven for 5 minutes.

☛ Bacon is much easier to chop and cut after it has been in the freezer for 20 minutes. The same goes for cheese; it's easier to grate when chilled.

☛ The next time you need room-temperature butter in a hurry, don't melt it; instead, grate it. The small pieces melt evenly in biscuits and pie dough and cream beautifully in cookies doughs and batters.

☛ Before making fresh whipped cream, place the metal bowl and beaters or whisk in the freezer; the cold metal results in faster whipped cream.

☛ When working with sweet potatoes, butternut squash, or raw pumpkin for soups or stews, cook them in the microwave for 3 minutes to make them easier to cut and/or peel.

☛ Save time and work more efficiently as you prep by placing a bowl on the counter for all the trash and scraps. When you are through, make just one trip to the trash can.

☛ Keep a freezer bag in the freezer for bread ends, stale hamburger buns, hot dog rolls, and any old bread pieces. Then, when you have a good amount, blitz the pieces in the food processor and make bread crumbs.

Reading Recipes

Understanding a recipe before you begin preparing the dish prevents mistakes, reduces waste, and ultimately saves time, tempting though it may be to rush ahead in your enthusiasm.

Before you do anything, read the *whole* recipe through . . . twice. If you are not familiar with a term or an ingredient, look it up (or use the index of this book). Trust that the order of the instructions are written that way for a reason. The prep time refers to how long it should take you to chop, mix, cut, and otherwise prepare the components of a recipe. The cook time refers to the time the food is actively cooking.

READING RECIPES IN THIS BOOK

The recipes in this book are all designed to be ready in 30 minutes or under, start to finish; a few dozen recipes can be made in 20 minutes or under.

The ingredients used in the recipes are available in the average grocery store. Some dishes are family favorites, some are particularly healthy, and a few are downright indulgent.

Some recipes include optional ingredients for garnishes that add a pop of color, taste, or texture to a finished dish. It's up to you whether you use them or not.

Often, I will call for a pinch of salt or pepper, or tell you to season "to taste." I like my food well-seasoned, but you're the cook in your kitchen: Use your judgment and as much or as little seasoning as you like. Just remember to "taste and adjust." You have to *taste* the food throughout the cooking process and *adjust* the seasonings accordingly for the best result.

Here are a few other recipe elements to be aware of:

Labels

Every recipe in this book includes one or more of the following labels.

1-Pot/Pan. Only one pot or pan is needed to cook these recipes, meaning less cleanup!

5-Ingredient. These recipes call for just five ingredients or fewer (excluding salt, pepper, and oil, if applicable).

Faster Than Delivery. This label indicates a recipe, e.g., pizza or takeout, that you would typically get delivered. By following the recipe, food will be on your table faster than if you ordered it from a restaurant!

Gluten-Free. This label indicates that no gluten is used in the recipe and is therefore suitable for those with gluten allergies, sensitivities, or celiac disease. Always check the ingredient labels on products before you buy, however, just to make sure the item is indeed Gluten-Free.

Vegetarian. Recipes with this label do not use meat, poultry, or seafood.

Tips

Many of the recipes in this book contain tips that may save you time, make you more efficient, or suggest alternate ways the dish can be enjoyed.

Got Leftovers? These tips suggest ways to repurpose leftovers.

Ingredient Tip. These tips give ways a component of a recipe may be used in other applications.

Pro Tip. These tips suggest ways to improve efficiency and avoid common mistakes.

Shopping Tip. These are suggestions for certain grocery store items that may shave prep time or enhance the flavor of the dish.

Swap It. These tips suggest how to make meatless dishes with meat or turn a nonvegetarian dish into a vegetarian dish. The tips also give ways to change up the flavor or protein in a recipe.

Take a Shortcut. These tips suggest ways you can make a dish more quickly, perhaps by using a canned, frozen, pre-made or pre-chopped version of an ingredient or using a certain piece of equipment.

How to Make More or Less

The recipes in this book can be easily halved or doubled to serve more or fewer people. When you want to alter the quantities, I recommend that you first read the recipe through and then write down the new quantity of ingredients *before* you begin to prep, cook, or bake. Don't rely on the numbers staying in your head. Keep in mind that halving a recipe that serves two may not be practical; you can always enjoy that second portion for the following day's lunch or dinner.

3

Breakfast

Breakfast Burritos

THESE BURRITOS ARE A GREAT WAY to start the day and can be easily customized by adding as many or as few additions as you wish. Running out the door? Wrap the burrito in aluminum foil and enjoy it on your journey to work or at your desk.

Serves: 2
Prep time: 5 minutes
Cook time: 5 minutes

4 eggs
½ tablespoon butter
Salt
Freshly ground black pepper
½ cup shredded
    Cheddar cheese
2 large tortillas
4 slices cooked bacon

1. Crack the eggs into a bowl and give them a quick whisk with a fork.
2. Heat a small frying pan or skillet over medium heat.
3. Add the butter to the pan. Tilt the pan to evenly coat it with the butter as it melts.
4. When the butter has melted, add the eggs and scramble them by gently turning them over with a small spatula until just cooked.
5. Season with salt and black pepper and remove from the heat.
6. Quickly sprinkle the Cheddar cheese down the center of each tortilla, top with the eggs and bacon, and wrap your burrito.

Got Leftovers? Make a double batch, cool, wrap individually in foil, and store in the refrigerator or freezer to enjoy a fast quality breakfast. They will store well in the refrigerator for up to 3 days; simply reheat in the microwave. Or store them in the freezer for up to 1 month; pop one out and thaw in the refrigerator overnight.

Swap It: Swap the bacon for sausage. Swap the Cheddar for your favorite cheese or spice it up with shredded Pepper Jack cheese. Add diced potatoes or cooked tater tots, or sautéed bell peppers, onions, or jalapeños.

Grapefruit Brûlée

FRUIT FOR BREAKFAST IS NEVER A BAD IDEA, and when the fruit is warm and decadent, even better! Use the broiler or toaster oven to easily transform an ordinary grapefruit into a warm and wonderful dish. This recipe also works as a snack or dessert.

Serves: 2
Prep time: 5 minutes
Cook time: 5 Minutes

1 large pink or white grapefruit
1 tablespoon sugar, preferably raw (see the Ingredient Tip)

1. Turn the oven's broiler to high and set the rack in the middle of the oven.
2. Wash and dry the grapefruit.
3. Cut a sliver from the top and bottom of the grapefruit, just enough so it can sit on a baking sheet without wobbling.
4. Cut the grapefruit in half horizontally.
5. Place each half cut-side down on a paper towel for 5 minutes.
6. Using a serrated knife, cut around the perimeter of the grapefruit, then around the edge of each segment so the segments will easily pop out with a spoon.
7. Remove any visible seeds.
8. Place the grapefruit halves on a baking sheet or in a small casserole dish and sprinkle evenly with the sugar.
9. Broil the grapefruit for 3 to 5 minutes until the sugar begins to caramelize (brown and bubble), then remove from the oven and serve immediately.

Got Leftovers? If you enjoy bourbon, try using the juice and/or a slice of brûléed grapefruit in a cocktail such as a Sidecar or Brown Derby. Adds amazing flavor!

Ingredient Tip: Raw sugar contains molasses, which gives it a light brown color and a rich flavor.

Mango Yogurt Smoothie

ONE OF MY DAUGHTER'S FAVORITE THINGS to make (and eat) is a homemade smoothie, whether it is for breakfast, a snack, or dessert. Need a fast breakfast on the go? Whip up a smoothie in just a few minutes and take it with you.

Serves: 2
Prep time: 5 minutes

1 cup plain yogurt

1 cup milk

1 banana

1 heaping cup frozen mango chunks

1 tablespoon honey (optional)

Combine all the ingredients in a blender and blend until smooth.

Ingredient Tip: You can use 2 fresh mangos in place of frozen. Pop a peeled banana in the freezer the night before for extra cold creaminess.

Swap It: Replace the mango with your favorite frozen berry or berry blend.

Pepper Egg Rings

THESE EGG RINGS ARE SIMPLE YET SATISFYING and a great way to start the day with veggies and protein. Love cheese? Shred a little Parmesan, Pepper Jack, or Cheddar over the top. Add a couple strips of bacon alongside or a slice of toast and you will be satisfied until lunchtime.

Serves: 2
Prep time: 5 minutes
Cook time: 5 minutes

1 large bell pepper, any color

Nonstick cooking spray

4 eggs

Salt

Freshly ground black pepper

Chopped fresh parsley,
   for garnish

1. Slice the bell pepper into four 1-inch-thick rings. Use a paring knife to clear the inside of each ring of any stems or seeds.
2. Heat a nonstick skillet over medium-high heat. Spray the skillet with cooking spray, add the pepper rings, and sauté them for 1 to 2 minutes, flipping them once.
3. Crack an egg into each pepper ring and cook to your liking, either sunny-side up or over easy.
4. Season with salt and black pepper, and sprinkle with the parsley.

Swap It: If you enjoy cheese on your eggs, sprinkle the rings with shredded Parmesan or Pepper Jack cheese, cover the skillet with a lid, and allow the cheese to melt.

Mini Ham and Cheese Breakfast Puffs

THESE PUFFS ARE ONE OF MY KIDS' FAVORITE BREAKFASTS. I love that I can easily customize them to what each of us enjoys. Whip up some of these breakfast puffs when you wake up, pop them in the oven while you shower, then take them out and enjoy a warm, low-carb, protein-filled breakfast to start your day off right.

Serves: 2
Prep time: 5 minutes
Cook time: 10 minutes

Nonstick cooking spray

3 eggs

2 tablespoons milk

Salt

Freshly ground black pepper

¼ cup shredded or chopped cheese (Cheddar, American, or Pepper Jack)

¼ cup diced ham

1. Preheat the oven to 375°F. Lightly coat a mini muffin pan with cooking spray.
2. In a mixing bowl, whisk together the eggs and milk.
3. Season with salt and black pepper and whisk again.
4. Fill each muffin cup halfway with the egg mixture.
5. Divide the ham and cheese between each cup, poking the meat and cheese down just a bit with a butter knife.
6. Bake for 8 to 10 minutes or until the eggs are set to your liking.
7. Remove the pan from the oven, gently run a butter knife around the edge of each cup, and serve.

Got Leftovers? Keep leftovers in a sealed container or resealable plastic bag in the refrigerator for up to 3 days; reheat in the microwave.

Swap It: Feel free to add scallions, onions, cooked bacon, cooked crumbled sausage, chopped spinach, or any of your favorite add-ins to these puffs. You can also make them in full-size cupcake tins; just increase the cooking time to 18 to 20 minutes.

Blueberry Pie Oatmeal

TAKE YOUR FAVORITE PLAIN OATMEAL TO THE NEXT LEVEL with this colorful breakfast. Besides the antioxidant benefit of blueberries, the combination of oatmeal and berry compote is absolutely delicious.

Serves: 2
Prep time: 2 minutes
Cook time: 10 minutes

---

2 servings your
    favorite oatmeal

1 cup fresh or frozen
    blueberries

1 tablespoon water

½ tablespoon freshly
    squeezed lemon juice

2 tablespoons sugar,
    or honey

Pinch ground cinnamon

1. Prepare two servings of your favorite oatmeal according to the package instructions.
2. In a small pot over high heat, combine the blueberries, water, lemon juice, sugar, and cinnamon.
3. Bring the mixture to a boil, then reduce the heat and simmer the compote, stirring it often. The berries will begin to pop; you don't need them all to pop, just about half.
4. After 5 or 6 minutes, remove the pot from the heat and spoon the compote onto the oatmeal. Then dig in!

Got Leftovers? This berry compote is wonderful over vanilla ice cream or stirred into plain yogurt.

Cheese Omelet

ONCE YOU MASTER MAKING THE HUMBLE CHEESE OMELET, you can experiment with just about any filling you can dream up. Top chefs say the perfect omelet has no brown parts and is still creamy, almost a little runny on the inside; however, once you nail the basic steps, you can customize yours however you like.

Serves: 1
Prep time: 5 minutes
Cook time: 5 minutes

2 eggs

½ tablespoon butter

Salt

Freshly ground black pepper

1 to 2 ounces grated cheese, such as Cheddar

1. Crack the eggs into a medium bowl, then vigorously whisk the eggs until they are one color and frothy. There should be no white patches in the mixture.
2. Heat an 8-inch nonstick pan over medium-low heat for about 30 seconds, then add the butter. You don't want too much heat here; the butter shouldn't make a sound when it hits the pan. Tilt the pan to evenly coat it with the butter as it melts.
3. Pour in the eggs, tilting the pan if necessary so the eggs completely cover the bottom of the pan. Let the eggs cook undisturbed until they are set.
4. Turn off the heat, quickly season the eggs with salt and black pepper, and scatter the cheese down the middle.
5. With a spatula, carefully lift one edge of the eggs and fold the omelet in half.
6. Allow the omelet to sit for another minute, remove it from the pan with a spatula, and serve.

Pro Tip: When cracking an egg, lightly crack it against the surface of the counter rather than against the edge of the bowl. This prevents eggshell bits from ending up in the eggs. To further perfect your omelet-making skills, I suggest going online and watching a chef make one. Watch, listen, and learn. There are American, French, and British omelet techniques. Find your favorite and practice until you perfect it.

Swap It: Try some of these fillings along with the cheese. Let your imagination—or last's night's leftovers—run wild!

- Sautéed kale or Swiss chard and crispy bacon
- Sautéed mushrooms and onions
- Scallions sautéed in butter
- Seasoned diced tomatoes
- Chopped ham, crumbled sausage, or bacon
- Fresh herbs such as chives, parsley, or tarragon.
- Instead of Cheddar, use Parmesan, crumbled feta, or goat cheese

Breakfast Banana Boats

THIS SIMPLE AND HEALTHY BREAKFAST is heartier than it may seem and can be enjoyed as a snack or dessert as well. If your mornings tend to be rushed, portion out the ingredients for this recipe the night before for easy grab-and-go, then assemble in the morning and eat at work or school.

Serves: 1
Prep time: 5 minutes

1 banana
½ cup yogurt
¼ cup granola
¼ cup your choice berries
Honey, for drizzling

1. Peel the banana, then cut it butterfly-style by running a knife down the length of the banana and pulling apart the two halves without fully separating them.
2. Top the banana with the yogurt, granola, berries, and a drizzle of honey.

Swap It: Enjoy this dish warm by placing the butterflied banana on aluminum foil and popping it under the broiler for a few minutes. Try spreading Nutella on the banana and sprinkling it with coconut flakes and chopped nuts.

Yogurt Pancakes

THESE TASTY PANCAKES CAN BE WHIPPED UP in just minutes. Customize them as you wish by adding chocolate chips or topping them with fresh fruit, fruit compote, whipped cream, or jam.

Makes: 4 pancakes
Prep time: 5 minutes
Cook time: 5 minutes

---

2 tablespoons butter

¼ cup vanilla yogurt

1 egg

1 tablespoon sugar

1 tablespoon water

¾ cup all-purpose flour

½ tablespoon baking powder

Pinch salt

Nonstick cooking
    spray or butter, for
    greasing the pan

1. In a medium bowl, whisk together the butter, yogurt, egg, sugar, and water. Set aside.
2. In a large bowl, whisk together the flour, baking powder, and salt.
3. Add the wet ingredients to the dry ingredients and mix until incorporated. Do not overmix; some lumps are okay.
4. Heat a nonstick skillet or griddle over medium heat until hot. Spray the skillet with cooking spray.
5. Pour about ⅓ cup of batter at a time into the skillet. Let it cook for about a minute and flip when a few bubbles start appearing (you can test the edge of the pancake with a spatula to see if it's firm and ready to flip).
6. Pancakes are done when they are browned on both sides, 2 to 3 minutes total per pancake.

Swap It: Add chocolate chips, banana pieces, or cinnamon and sugar.

Granola Berry Bowl

PREPARING BREAKFAST DOES NOT HAVE TO BE TIME-CONSUMING. This super easy berry-filled bowl is a simple 5-minute breakfast. Serve as is with milk, over yogurt or a smoothie, or as a topping for your favorite overnight oats.

Serves: 2
Prep time: 5 minutes

2 granola bars, broken into pieces (or 1 cup granola)

1 cup sliced strawberries, blackberries, blueberries, or berry mixture

1 banana, sliced

Honey, for drizzling

½ cup milk (optional)

In a mixing bowl, combine the granola pieces, berries, and banana. Divide the mixture between 2 serving bowls, drizzle with honey, and serve with the milk (if using).

Swap It: Turn this into a smoothie bowl. Pour your favorite smoothie or yogurt into a bowl and top with the granola, berries, and banana. You can also add coconut flakes, pepitas, or hemp seeds.

Cheesy Grits and Sausage

WHEN YOU WAKE UP HUNGRY and crave a warm and robust breakfast, you can make it happen fast with this cheesy, creamy dish. It's like a hug in a bowl.

Serves: 2
Prep time: 5 minutes
Cook time: 10 minutes

5 ounces loose chorizo

2 cups milk

½ cup quick-cooking grits

Pinch salt

⅛ teaspoon freshly ground black pepper

⅓ cup shredded mozzarella cheese

⅔ cup shredded Cheddar cheese, Monterey Jack, or Pepper Jack

1 scallion, green part only, finely chopped, for garnish

1. In a medium pan over medium heat, cook the chorizo until browned and cooked through, about 7 minutes. Transfer the chorizo to a bowl, blot any grease with a paper towel, and set aside.
2. In a saucepan over medium-high heat, bring the milk to a simmer and whisk in the grits, salt, and black pepper.
3. Stir vigorously for 4 minutes or until the grits thicken.
4. Stir in the cooked chorizo and the mozzarella and Cheddar cheeses and stir for a minute until the cheeses melt.
5. Divide the mixture between 2 serving bowls and sprinkle with the scallion.

Shopping Tip: To save 5 minutes or so, you can buy cooked chorizo. Simply sauté it for a minute or two in a hot pan with just a bit of oil or cooking spray to warm it through.

Avocado Breakfast Toast

HERE'S THE THING ABOUT AVOCADO TOAST: It's so versatile you can take it to any level you want. Load it up or dress it simply. Make it meatless, top it with any type of egg, vegetable, or meat—there are no rules. Enjoy it for breakfast, lunch, dinner, or as a snack.

Serves: 2
Prep time: 5 minutes
Cook time: 5 minutes

---

1 avocado

Freshly squeezed lime juice

Salt

Freshly ground black pepper

1 tablespoon olive oil
or butter

2 eggs

2 slices whole grain bread
(or your favorite), toasted

1. With a sharp knife, cut the avocado lengthwise all the way around the pit, then twist apart the two halves.
2. To remove the pit, gently hit the pit with the sharp edge of the knife, just enough so the knife catches and you can twist the pit out of the avocado and discard it.
3. Scoop the flesh out with a spoon and discard the skins.
4. On a cutting board or in a bowl, slice or mash the avocado and season it well with lime juice, salt, and black pepper. Set aside.
5. Heat a nonstick pan over medium-high heat and pour in the olive oil.
6. Crack the eggs into the pan and cook for about 3 minutes or until the whites are set.
7. Arrange the avocado on the toasted bread and top each slice with a fried egg. For something more robust, add any of the optional toppings.

Optional toppings: Crumbled bacon, chives, scallions, pine nuts, pepitas, goat cheese, Cotija cheese, feta cheese, sliced red onion, diced jalapeño, sliced radish, arugula, sprouts, micro greens, etc.

4

Snacks and Sides

Chocolate Oatmeal Energy Bites

THESE NO-BAKE BITES ARE EASY to make and can be customized in a variety of ways. They are perfect for keeping in the freezer for when a sweet craving strikes but you want to get the benefit of some protein instead of just empty calories from candy.

Makes: 20 bites
Prep time: 15 minutes

1½ cups old fashioned oats
½ ripe banana
½ cup peanut butter
¼ cup honey
½ teaspoon vanilla extract
2 tablespoons raisins
3 tablespoons mini
   chocolate chips

1. Combine the oats and banana in a mixing bowl and mix them together using a potato masher. You can use an entire banana if you like; just add a bit more oatmeal if necessary because banana sizes vary.
2. In a microwave-safe bowl, microwave the peanut butter and honey together for 15 to 20 seconds, just enough to make them a bit easier to incorporate.
3. Add the peanut butter mixture, vanilla extract, raisins, and chocolate chips to the bowl with the banana and oats and mix until all the ingredients are well combined.
4. Form the mixture into balls, pressing very firmly until they're round and compact. If you have extra time, cover the bowl and place it in the refrigerator for 30 minutes or more before forming the mixture into balls (it will be less sticky if you do this).
5. Place the bites on a baking sheet and let them sit for about 2 hours to dry up a bit.
6. Store the bites in an airtight container in the refrigerator for up to 4 days or in the freezer in freezer bags. Pull out a few whenever the mood hits for a snack. They will thaw in 20 minutes or less.

Swap It: Change it up. Swap out creamy peanut butter for crunchy peanut butter. Add some Nutella for more chocolate flavor. Swap raisins for cranberries. Add chia seeds, hemp seeds, sunflower seeds, or pepitas. Allergic to nuts? Swap peanut butter for sesame butter or another favorite nut-free spread. Swap agave or maple syrup for honey. There is no right or wrong when making these.

Sweet and Spicy Nuts

YOU KNOW HOW PEOPLE TEND TO GET "FAMOUS" in their circles of family and friends for something they make, such as a cocktail, appetizer, or barbecue dish? These nuts are one of those things; people go crazy for them. Enjoy them as a snack, on salads, on flatbreads, or break them up and scatter on top of whipped ricotta (my favorite). You'll definitely want to make several batches, wrap them up pretty, and give them as gifts come the holidays.

Serves: 4
Prep time: 5 minutes
Cook time: 10 minutes

¼ teaspoon kosher salt

¼ teaspoon ground cinnamon

Pinch cayenne pepper

Nonstick cooking spray

1 cup sugar

2½ cups nuts (walnuts, pecans, or almonds)

1. In a small bowl, stir together the salt, cinnamon, and cayenne and set aside.
2. Line a baking sheet with parchment paper and spray lightly with cooking spray.
3. In a heavy pot or large saucepan over medium heat, pan roast the nuts for about 3 minutes, stirring the whole time. Transfer them to a bowl and set aside.
4. Put the sugar in the pot, still over medium heat, and allow it to melt, stirring often with a silicone spatula or wooden spoon. Do not allow the sugar to burn. Keep it moving, pulling the sides of the sugar toward the middle over and over, for 5 to 8 minutes, until it is similar in texture and color to maple syrup.
5. Add the nuts, followed immediately by the spice mixture, and stir quickly.
6. Turn off the heat and quickly flip the nuts onto the prepared baking sheet.
7. Use 2 forks to quickly pull the nuts apart. They will harden quickly and become similar to peanut brittle.
8. Allow the nuts to cool completely. Once cooled, you can break them apart more if you like. Store in an airtight container.

Herbed Pita Chips

THESE CHIPS ARE A SIMPLE SNACK you may find yourself making again and again. Enjoy them on their own, as part of a cheese or charcuterie board, or with your favorite dip. They're also delicious crumbled over salads and soups.

Serves: 3 to 4
Prep time: 10 minutes
Cook time: 10 minutes

4 pita breads

3 tablespoons olive oil

½ teaspoon garlic powder

½ teaspoon dried basil, thyme, or Italian seasoning

¼ teaspoon freshly ground black pepper

Salt (optional)

1. Preheat the oven to 375°F. Line a baking sheet with parchment paper.
2. Cut the pitas into slices like a pizza pie.
3. In a small bowl, combine the olive oil, garlic powder, basil, and pepper. Stir to combine.
4. Brush the seasoned oil onto both sides of the pita wedges and place the wedges on the baking sheet.
5. Bake for 8 to 10 minutes or until crisp.
6. Remove from the oven and immediately sprinkle the chips with salt (if using).

Got Leftovers? These chips keep in an airtight container or resealable plastic bag for up to 1 week.

Swap It: You can use fresh ingredients to season the oil as well, such as garlic paste, minced garlic, and fresh herbs. Just let them sit in the oil for at least 10 minutes before using. If salt is not a concern, you can also salt the oil mixture for added flavor. You can cut the pitas into strips instead of wedges. For crispier chips, separate the pitas down the middle; the chips will be thinner and yield twice as many.

Bacon Guacamole

WE ALL KNOW THAT GUACAMOLE IS GOOD, but bacon guacamole? Even better! Change up your guac game by adding some crispy bacon bits. This guacamole is great for snacking, as a party appetizer, or as a topping on burgers. Never had a guacamole-topped burger? You really should!

Serves: 4
Prep time: 10 minutes

3 avocados, pitted and skins removed

Salt

Freshly ground black pepper

1 teaspoon freshly squeezed lime juice

1 jalapeño pepper, chopped

1 tablespoon garlic paste, or 1 garlic clove, mashed and minced

5 pieces crispy cooked bacon, crumbled

½ cup grape tomatoes, chopped

3 scallions, thinly sliced

Optional add-ins: chopped cilantro to taste, red pepper for added heat, or minced onion.

1. Place the avocado flesh in a medium bowl and season well with salt and black pepper. Add the lime juice and mash the avocados with the back of a fork or potato masher.
2. Add the jalapeño pepper (for extra heat, leave in the seeds), garlic paste, bacon, tomatoes, and scallions (as well as any add-ins you may choose) and mix with a fork or a spoon until well incorporated.
3. Taste and adjust the seasonings.
4. Serve with tortilla chips.

Pro Tip: If making ahead, cover guacamole tightly with plastic wrap, pressing it right against the top of the guacamole. Air is what makes avocados turn brown. Guacamole is best enjoyed the day you make it.

10-Minute Salsa

THIS IS SERIOUSLY THE BEST SALSA, EVER. Once you make this, you will become known for it. Even better, it's just so easy and economical. Make it your own by adding more or less of the ingredients listed. Enjoy hot and spicy food? Add an extra jalapeño or red pepper flakes. You can make this salsa as mild or as hot as you like.

Makes: about 3½ cups
Prep time: 10 minutes

1 (28-ounce) can whole fire-roasted tomatoes

1 jalapeño pepper

2 large garlic cloves, cut into thirds

½ cup chopped fresh cilantro

2 tablespoons freshly squeezed lime juice

2 to 3 tablespoons honey

¾ teaspoon salt

½ teaspoon ground cumin

Combine all the ingredients in a blender or food processor and pulse until smooth. Taste and adjust the seasoning to your liking.

Swap It: Enjoy onions in your salsa? Feel free to add a few slices. To give the salsa an extra kick, leave in some or all of the jalapeño seeds and stems, or add a pinch of cayenne.

Take a Shortcut: No food processor or blender? No problem. Buy a can of crushed tomatoes (fire-roasted if available), then simply mince the rest of the ingredients with a chef's knife. Whisk vigorously or shake in a sealed container to combine.

Hummus and Veggie Flatbread

THIS SIMPLE FLATBREAD MAKES A FANTASTIC SNACK, appetizer, or light lunch. You can customize this by adding or swapping ingredients such as sliced bell peppers, chopped artichokes, crispy seasoned chickpeas, or even crispy Brussels sprout quarters. You can typically find naan flatbread in the bakery or deli section of the grocery store. Sizes may vary, but one large piece or two medium pieces of naan work great for this recipe.

Serves: 2
Prep time: 10 minutes
Cook time: 5 minutes

1 (8- to 10-inch) naan or
    4 smaller flatbreads

Olive oil

Salt

Freshly ground black pepper

1 cup homemade or store-
    bought hummus

⅓ cup chopped cucumber

⅓ cup grape
    tomatoes, halved

⅓ cup Kalamata olives

⅓ cup crumbled feta cheese

Chopped fresh parsley,
    for garnish

1. Preheat the oven to 375°F.
2. Lightly brush the flatbread with olive oil on both sides and season the top side with salt and black pepper. Place on a baking sheet and bake for 4 to 5 minutes or until the edges begin to crisp and brown.
3. Allow the flatbread to cool for a few minutes, then spread it with the hummus. Add the cucumber, tomatoes, olives, and feta cheese. Garnish with chopped parsley.
4. Cut into slices or strips and enjoy.

Ingredient Tip: It literally takes just minutes to make your own hummus. Give it a try. All you need are: 1 (15-ounce) can good quality chickpeas, ¼ cup tahini, 2 large garlic cloves, 2 tablespoons olive oil, 2 tablespoons water, 2½ tablespoons freshly squeezed lemon juice, 1 teaspoon salt, and ¼ teaspoon ground cumin. Drain and rinse the chickpeas in a colander and set aside. Combine the remaining ingredients in a food processor and process until smooth. Add the chickpeas and process for 2 to 3 minutes until smooth and creamy.

Shopping Tip: Hummus is typically found in the deli section near the cheese cases. There are so many flavors available that would work with this recipe—plain, roasted red pepper, garlic. Take your pick!

Sautéed Spinach

ONE OF THE ORIGINAL SUPERFOODS, spinach is loaded with vitamins and minerals, is low in calories, and is delicious raw in salads or cooked in soups as well as in this super easy recipe, which can be cooked in 5 minutes flat.

Serves: 2
Prep time: 5 minutes
Cook time: 5 minutes

1 (10-ounce) bag fresh baby spinach

1 tablespoon olive oil

1 large garlic clove, minced

¼ teaspoon salt

¼ teaspoon freshly ground black pepper

Freshly squeezed lemon juice

1. Rinse the spinach in a colander under cold water, then blot dry with paper towels or, if you have one, dry using a salad spinner.
2. Heat a large pot over medium-high heat and pour in the olive oil. Add the garlic and sauté for 1 minute, moving it around and being careful to not burn it.
3. Quickly add the spinach, season it with the salt and black pepper, and pack it down with a spatula.
4. Use the spatula to stir the spinach around, ensuring it cooks evenly, until it is wilted, about 2 minutes.
5. Remove from the heat, spritz with lemon juice, and season with a little more salt and black pepper if you like.

Pro Tip: Spinach may look like it will yield a lot, but you'll be surprised every time by how much it cooks down. Always use a large pot so the leaves don't fly out when you first start cooking.

Swap It: Sprinkle spinach with freshly shredded Parmesan or drizzle with just a little balsamic vinegar.

Perfect Mashed Potatoes

AS A SIDE DISH, GOOD MASHED POTATOES ARE HARD TO BEAT. They are the epitome of comfort food. Once you master the basics of mashed potatoes, you can add tasty ingredients such as cheese, roasted garlic, sautéed scallions or leeks, or even browned butter for a deliciously nutty taste.

Serves: 4
Prep time: 10 minutes
Cook time: 15 minutes

1½ pounds Russet or Yukon Gold potatoes, peeled and cut into even chunks

2 heaping teaspoons salt, divided

3 tablespoons butter

½ cup milk

⅛ teaspoon freshly ground black pepper

1. Put the potatoes in a large pot, then add just enough water to cover them. Add 1 teaspoon of salt to the water.
2. Boil the potatoes until they are easily pierced with a fork, about 15 minutes.
3. While they are boiling, heat the butter in a saucepan over medium heat for about 1 minute, or in a microwave-safe bowl in the microwave for about 30 seconds.
4. Heat the milk in a saucepan over medium heat for about 1 minute, or in a microwave-safe bowl in the microwave for about 30 seconds, until hot but not boiling.
5. Drain the potatoes and return them to the pot. Place the pot over low heat for about 2 minutes to dry the potatoes, moving them around every 30 seconds.
6. Remove the pot from the heat and mash the potatoes with a potato masher. Add the hot milk, soft/melted butter, remaining 1 teaspoon of salt, and black pepper and stir with a spatula until combined. Taste and adjust the seasoning if necessary. Add additional milk as needed to get your desired consistency.

Got Leftovers? Make loaded skillet potatoes: Coat a cast iron skillet or nonstick sauté pan with olive oil, press the potatoes into the skillet, and top with shredded cheese, crumbled bacon, and chopped scallions. You can also choose to stir in some sour cream and cheese into the potatoes before placing them in the skillet. Cook over medium heat for 8 to 10 minutes until heated through and the cheese has melted.

Pro Tip: For the fluffiest mashed potatoes, make sure they are dry before mashing and use either a potato ricer or a hand masher. Never use an electric mixer to make mashed potatoes or you will end up with gummy potatoes.

Asian-Style Green Beans

THE INSPIRATION FOR THESE GREEN BEANS comes from one of my favorite Asian restaurants. I love how the sauce coats the crisp-tender beans. Enjoy this as a side dish paired with just about any meat or as part of a meatless meal. You can easily control how mild or spicy you make this dish as well.

Serves: 4
Prep time: 10 minutes
Cook time: 10 minutes

2 tablespoons low-sodium soy sauce

1 tablespoon rice wine vinegar

1 teaspoon sugar

1 teaspoon cornstarch

2 tablespoons sesame oil

3 garlic cloves, minced

½ teaspoon red pepper flakes

1 pound fresh green beans, rinsed and ends trimmed (see Ingredient Tip)

1. In a small bowl, mix together the soy sauce, rice wine vinegar, sugar, and cornstarch. Set aside.
2. In a large skillet or sauté pan (or wok if you have one) over medium heat, heat the sesame oil for about 30 seconds. Add the garlic and red pepper flakes, and cook for 30 seconds, stirring constantly.
3. Add the green beans and cook until crisp-tender, 3 to 5 minutes depending on the size of the beans. If you prefer softer beans, cook them for a couple minutes longer.
4. Pour the soy sauce mixture into the skillet and stir for another 1 to 2 minutes to coat the green beans and slightly thicken the sauce. Remove from the heat and serve.

Ingredient Tip: To trim green beans, you can snap the ends off with your fingers or cut them off with a knife or kitchen shears.

Herb Roasted Mushrooms

ROASTING MUSHROOMS BRINGS OUT THEIR NUTTY FLAVOR. These mushrooms are so rich and tasty that those in your life who think they don't like mushrooms may just change their mind. Serve these alongside meat, and if a vegetarian is coming to dinner, make extra!

Serves: 4
Prep time: 5 minutes
Cook time: 25 minutes

1½ pounds whole small mushrooms (button, baby portabella, or shiitake)

1 tablespoon olive oil

Kosher salt

Freshly ground black pepper

2 tablespoons butter

2 tablespoons minced garlic

½ teaspoon paprika

½ teaspoon fresh thyme leaves

1. Preheat the oven to 425°F.
2. Put the mushrooms in a 13-by-9-inch casserole dish or on a baking sheet, drizzle with the olive oil, season well with salt and black pepper, and, using your hands, mix well until the mushrooms are fully coated.
3. Roast the mushrooms for 20 to 25 minutes until they are browned in spots and tender, removing the dish from the oven once or twice to toss the mushrooms with a spatula.
4. While the mushrooms cook, combine the butter, garlic, paprika, and thyme in a small pot or pan and sauté for 2 minutes over medium-low heat.
5. Remove the seasoned butter from the heat.
6. Place the roasted mushrooms in a serving dish, pour the seasoned butter on top, toss to combine, and sprinkle with additional salt and black pepper if desired.

Oven-Roasted Asparagus

WHEN I WAS A KID, my parents must have boiled their asparagus, because I just didn't want to eat it (even though it often came right from my dad's huge garden). However, once I began roasting asparagus at a high temperature, and its slightly nutty flavor came out, I was smitten. This is one vegetable my whole family loves.

Serves: 3 to 4
Prep time: 2 minutes
Cook time: 15 minutes

---

1 bunch asparagus (1¼ to 1½ pounds)
½ tablespoon olive oil
Kosher salt
Freshly ground black pepper

1. Preheat the oven to 425°F.
2. Cut or snap off the ends of the asparagus (roughly the bottom inch) and discard.
3. Place the asparagus on a baking sheet, with all the tips facing the same way. Drizzle with the olive oil, and season well with salt and pepper. Using your hands or a spatula, mix until the asparagus are evenly coated.
4. Bake for 10 to 15 minutes. The thicker the asparagus, the longer it will take. If the asparagus is very thin, reduce the oven temperature to 400°F.

Swap It: Season the oil with some minced garlic or garlic paste, or sprinkle the asparagus with shredded Parmesan just as it comes out of the oven.

Drop Biscuits

WARM BISCUITS STRAIGHT FROM THE OVEN are delicious with soups, chili, salads, and many meats. They also make for a wonderful snack and can be used to make breakfast or lunch sandwiches. Easily customize this recipe using your favorite cheese, such as Cheddar, a Cheddar blend, Pepper Jack, or Parmesan.

Makes: 6 large biscuits
Prep time: 5 minutes
Cook time: 20 minutes

4 tablespoons cold butter, cut into small pieces

1 cup all-purpose flour

½ tablespoon baking powder

¼ teaspoon baking soda

Pinch salt

Pinch freshly ground black pepper

Pinch sugar

¾ cup shredded cheese

¼ cup thinly sliced scallions

½ cup milk

1. Preheat the oven to 400°F. Line a baking sheet with parchment paper, or lightly grease the baking sheet with nonstick cooking spray.
2. In a bowl, combine the butter, flour, baking powder, and baking soda.
3. Blend the mixture with a pastry cutter, fork, or your fingertips until crumbly. You could also blend these ingredients in a food processor.
4. Add the salt, black pepper, sugar, cheese, and scallions, tossing to combine.
5. Make a well in the center of the mixture, pour in the milk, and gently stir it together until just combined. Do not overmix.
6. Using an ice cream scoop (which measures ¼ cup), drop scoops of batter onto the prepared baking sheet, leaving 2 inches of space between biscuits.
7. Bake until lightly golden brown, 15 to 18 minutes.

Swap It: Add diced or chopped ham for ham and cheese biscuits. Add chopped jalapeños, red pepper flakes, or a pinch of cayenne for a little kick.

Take a Shortcut: Save time and use pre-shredded cheese.

5

Sandwiches, Salads, and Bowls

Chicken Salad Wraps

A FEW YEARS AGO, I HAPPENED UPON a popular breakfast spot while visiting Atlantic City. Everyone ordered breakfast; however, I only had eyes for their number one dish, their famous chicken salad. I replicated it at home, and now it's my go-to and a family favorite. Enjoy in a wrap, in a pita, or on bread or a roll. I often put a couple scoops atop salad greens and enjoy it as a low-carb lunch.

Serves: 2
Prep time: 10 minutes

1 celery stalk, cut into
   3 pieces

4 baby carrots, halved

2 heaping cups roughly
   chopped cooked chicken
   (about 2 boneless
   chicken breasts)

6 tablespoons mayonnaise

1½ tablespoons honey

Pinch salt

Freshly ground black pepper

2 flour tortillas

Romaine lettuce (optional)

Crispy cooked bacon slices
   (optional)

1. Combine the celery and carrots in a food processor or high-powered blender and pulse a few times until they are chopped small. Add the chicken pieces, mayonnaise, honey, salt, and black pepper, and pulse a few times until all the ingredients are chopped and incorporated.
2. Scrape the mixture into a bowl.
3. Taste and add more mayonnaise if desired to get the salad to the texture you enjoy and adjust the seasoning to your liking. Mix well.
4. Spread the salad on the tortillas, add lettuce and bacon (if using), and wrap the tortillas up burrito-style.

Shopping Tip: If your grocery store sells rotisserie chicken or freshly grilled or fried chicken, pick some up to make this chicken salad.

Hot Ham and Swiss

KICK YOUR TYPICAL HAM AND CHEESE SANDWICH up a notch! This sandwich has a satisfying crunch, is full of flavors, and pairs wonderfully with the Perfect Tomato Soup (page 74). Cook this tasty sandwich in a frying pan or griddle or, if you have one, use a panini maker or countertop grill press for an even faster finish.

Serves: 2
Prep time: 5 minutes
Cook time: 10 minutes

---

2 tablespoons butter, at room temperature

4 slices white or whole grain bread

1½ teaspoons mayonnaise

1½ teaspoons whole grain mustard

6 slices deli ham or leftover ham

4 slices Swiss cheese

1. Spread the butter on one side of all 4 slices of bread.
2. Spread the mayonnaise and mustard on the unbuttered side of 2 pieces of bread, then top with the ham and Swiss cheese. Top each with the remaining 2 slices of bread, buttered side facing outward, to make 2 sandwiches.
3. Heat a frying pan over medium heat.
4. Once the pan is hot, place the sandwiches in the pan and cook for about 3 minutes per side or until the bread is crisp and golden.
5. Plate the sandwiches, slice in half, and serve.

Ingredient Tip: Add slices of pickle, arugula, baby spinach, or even thin slices of green apples to the sandwich.

Grown-Up Grilled Cheese

I BET MOST ADULTS WOULD AGREE that the most comforting sandwich is the humble grilled cheese. After all, for most of us it was a staple growing up. Elevate your next grilled cheese with artisan bread, Brie cheese, and jam. You may never go back to the original.

Serves: 2
Prep time: 5 minutes
Cook time: 5 minutes

---

1 tablespoon butter, at room temperature

4 slices sourdough or ciabatta bread (just about any artisan bread will work)

4 tablespoons fig jam

6 ounces sliced Brie cheese, rinds removed

Fresh chopped thyme leaves (optional)

1 Granny Smith apple, thinly sliced (optional)

1. Spread the butter on one side of all 4 slices of bread.
2. Spread the inside of 2 slices of bread liberally with the fig jam and top with the Brie cheese, thyme, and apple slices (if using). Top each with the remaining 2 slices of bread, buttered side facing outward, to make 2 sandwiches.
3. Heat a large pan or cast iron skillet over medium-high heat.
4. Place the sandwiches in the pan and lower the heat to medium. Cook for about 2 minutes per side until the cheese is melted and the bread is crisp and golden.
5. Plate the sandwiches, slice in half, and serve.

Swap It: You can add crispy bacon to the sandwich or swap out the fig jam for your favorite fruit preserve or honey. If you have a panini maker, you can use it to make these panini-style.

Italian Chicken Sandwiches

PHILLY IS KNOWN FOR CHEESESTEAKS; however, the other two sandwiches it should be known for are the roast pork sandwich and the Italian chicken sandwich. A stroll through Philly's famous Reading Terminal will have you wanting to order all three. This one is my favorite. Once you know how to prepare and cook broccoli rabe, you'll enjoy it as a wonderful side to meats as well as in these sandwiches.

Serves: 2
Prep time: 10 minutes
Cook time: 10 minutes

Salt

1 medium bunch broccoli rabe, stems removed

Olive oil

2 garlic cloves, roughly chopped

Pinch red pepper flakes

Freshly ground black pepper

1 egg, beaten

½ cup fine bread crumbs

2 thin boneless chicken breasts

2 roasted red bell peppers, cut into strips

½ cup shaved Parmesan cheese

2 seeded Italian or hoagie rolls

1. Fill a small pot with water, add a large pinch of salt, and bring the water to a boil over high heat.
2. Fill a large bowl with ice water and add a large pinch of salt.
3. Add the broccoli rabe to the boiling water and cook for 1 minute.
4. Quickly strain the broccoli rabe and immediately transfer it to the ice bath. Once the broccoli rabe is cool, strain it and pat dry.
5. Heat a large pan or skillet over medium heat and pour in just enough olive oil to lightly coat the bottom.
6. Add the garlic and red pepper flakes to the pan. Cook for about 1 minute, then add the broccoli rabe and season with salt and pepper. All you're doing here is seasoning the vegetable, because it's already cooked. Toss the broccoli rabe for about 2 minutes, then transfer it to a plate. Remove the pan from the heat.
7. Put the egg in one shallow dish and the bread crumbs in a separate shallow dish.
8. First, dip 1 chicken piece in the egg to coat it. Let any excess egg drip off the chicken, then dredge the chicken in the bread crumbs to thoroughly coat it. Set aside. Repeat with the second piece of chicken.
9. Return the pan to medium heat and pour some more oil into the pan to recoat the bottom. When the oil starts to shimmer, add the breaded chicken cutlets and cook for 3 to 4 minutes per side until crisped and cooked through.
10. Assemble the sandwiches by layering half the chicken, broccoli rabe, bell peppers, and Parmesan cheese in each roll.

Caesar Salad

SURE, YOU CAN USE STORE-BOUGHT CAESAR DRESSING, but why not make your own? You can whip up a perfect dressing in less than 10 minutes. Enjoy this classic salad plain, or add a protein such as grilled or breaded chicken, salmon, or blackened shrimp.

Serves: 4
Prep time: 10 minutes
Cook time: 5 minutes

2 large eggs

4 canned anchovy fillets

2 garlic cloves

1 tablespoon Worcestershire sauce

½ tablespoon capers, drained

½ tablespoon grainy Dijon mustard (Grey Poupon Country Dijon is great)

2 tablespoons red wine vinegar

2 tablespoons grated Parmesan cheese, plus more for garnish

¼ cup olive oil

1 teaspoon Tabasco sauce

1 head romaine lettuce, leaves separated, rinsed, and spun or blotted dry

Croutons

Freshly ground black pepper

Optional toppings: grape tomatoes, halved, 2 hardboiled eggs, 1 grilled or breaded chicken breast

1. Bring a pot of water to a boil over high heat and, using a large serving spoon, quickly and carefully lower in the eggs. Let them boil for exactly 2½ minutes, take them out, and run them under cold water for 30 seconds.
2. Using a butter knife, cut off the top 20 percent of the egg and pour the yolk into a food processor or blender. Discard the rest of the egg.
3. Add the anchovies, garlic, Worcestershire sauce, capers, mustard, red wine vinegar, and Parmesan cheese. Pulse or blend until smooth. Slowly pour in the olive oil while the processor runs or, if using a blender, add the oil gradually between pulses. Finally, add the Tabasco and pulse or blend until smooth and creamy.
4. Chop or tear the romaine leaves into bite-size pieces and place in a large serving bowl. Add the croutons, pour over the dressing, and toss to coat.
5. Sprinkle with additional shaved Parmesan cheese and pepper. Top with any or all of the optional toppings.

Swap It: For a nice twist, oil, and preheat the grill. Once the grill is hot, lay whole spears of romaine lettuce directly on the grill for a couple minutes, just until slightly charred and wilted.

Crispy Avocado Bacon and Tomato Salad

THE COMBINATION OF FLAVORS AND TEXTURES in this recipe makes this one of my favorite salads. I love making a quick two-ingredient dressing to go with it. You can choose to toss the greens with a store-bought lemon or lime vinaigrette, then drizzle the avocados with the spicy ranch dressing. If you're not in the mood for a salad, simply make the crispy avocados and snack away.

Serves: 2
Prep time: 10 minutes
Cook time: 5 minutes

1 (16-ounce) bag
    mixed greens

1 tomato, sliced

1 avocado

Pinch salt

Freshly ground black pepper

1 egg, beaten

⅓ cup all-purpose flour

½ cup panko bread crumbs

2 tablespoons grated
    Parmesan cheese, plus
    shaved Parmesan,
    for serving

Olive oil

⅓ cup ranch dressing

1 teaspoon sriracha

3 pieces crispy bacon,
    crumbled, for serving

1. Put the greens and tomato slices in a bowl or on a serving dish and set aside.

2. With a sharp knife, cut the avocado lengthwise all the way around the pit, then twist apart the two halves. To remove the pit, gently hit it with the sharp edge of the knife, just enough so the knife catches, then twist the pit out of the avocado and discard it.

3. Slice each avocado half into wedges. You should be able to get about 4 wedges from each half. Don't slice them too thinly; you want them to hold up to the breading and frying. Sprinkle the wedges with a bit of salt and black pepper.

4. Crack the egg into a small bowl and stir with a whisk or fork until the white and yolk are combined. Set aside.

5. Place the flour in a shallow bowl. In another bowl, mix together the panko bread crumbs and grated Parmesan cheese.

6. Dredge each piece of avocado in the flour and gently shake off any excess flour. Then dip the pieces in the egg mixture and then into the panko mixture, coating all sides well. Set aside.

7. Heat a large skillet or sauté pan over medium-high heat. Pour just enough olive oil into the pan to lightly cover the bottom, about ⅛ inch deep.

8. Once the oil is beginning to shimmer, use a slotted spatula or spoon to carefully place the avocado pieces in the skillet one at a time. Don't crowd the pieces; fry in batches if necessary.
9. Fry the wedges on each side until crisp and browned, 1½ to 2 minutes.
10. Use the slotted spatula or spoon to transfer the wedges to a paper towel–lined plate.
11. In a small bowl, make the dressing by mixing together the ranch dressing and sriracha.
12. Place the fried avocado slices on top of the salad, sprinkle with the crumbled bacon and shaved Parmesan cheese, drizzle with the dressing, and serve.

Kale Salad

MY NIECE CAME HOME FROM SCHOOL one day in 6th grade, excited to tell us about a recipe she'd learned; her school had a program where once a month, college students would come to teach the kids a simple, healthy recipe, and that day they taught her how to make this salad. She loved it so much that she made it for us that night. It's simple, satisfying, and healthy, and I've loved it ever since.

Serves: 4
Prep time: 15 minutes

1 (8-ounce) bunch or bag of kale, washed and dried

3 tablespoons olive oil

1½ tablespoons balsamic vinegar

1 tablespoon freshly squeezed lemon juice

2½ tablespoons honey

Pinch salt

Freshly ground black pepper

¾ cup dried cranberries

⅓ cup shelled sunflower seeds

4 to 6 ounces goat cheese, crumbled

1 small red onion, halved and thinly sliced (optional)

1. Remove the thick, hard stems of the kale either by slicing the leaves off either side of the stems or by tearing apart the leaves with your hands. Discard the stems.
2. Chop or tear the kale into bite-size pieces, put in a bowl, and set aside.
3. In a large mason jar or bowl, combine the olive oil, balsamic vinegar, lemon juice, and honey and season with salt and black pepper. Shake or whisk the mixture vigorously until combined.
4. Taste the dressing and adjust the seasoning to your preference for sweet versus tangy.
5. Pour half the dressing onto the kale. Then, with clean hands, massage the kale. Really work it in. You want to massage the leaves for about 2 minutes. This will transform the kale, softening it and turning it a darker green color.
6. Add the cranberries, sunflower seeds, goat cheese, and red onion (if using).
7. Drizzle with the remaining dressing, toss, and serve.

Pro Tip: Massaging the kale is key, so don't skip this step. If you have kids, even very young ones, enlist them for this part. They love getting their hands into food—plus, they most likely will at least try a dish they helped prepare. This salad holds up well and can be enjoyed the following day.

Greek Orzo Salad

THIS GREEK PASTA SALAD IS LIGHT and full of flavor. It's fantastic for lunch or as a side dish and is easily transportable. It keeps well for three to five days in a sealed container in the refrigerator. Make extra dressing if you plan on enjoying this for more than one day, as the pasta tends to soak it up while it sits.

Serves: 4
Prep time: 15 minutes
Cook time: 10 minutes

1 cup orzo pasta

½ cup olive oil, divided

2 tablespoons Greek seasoning (see Ingredient Tip)

1 teaspoon freshly squeezed lemon juice

1 cup pitted Kalamata olives

1 cup chopped cucumber

1 cup grape tomatoes, halved

½ cup feta cheese, crumbled

½ cup chopped fresh parsley

1 cup chopped artichoke hearts (optional)

1. In a medium pot, cook the orzo according to the package instructions.
2. Drain the orzo in a colander and run it under cold water to cool it. Blot some of the moisture with paper towels.
3. Transfer the orzo to a serving bowl and toss with 2 tablespoons of olive oil.
4. In a mason jar or small mixing bowl, combine the remaining 2 tablespoons of olive oil, Greek seasoning, and lemon juice. Shake or whisk vigorously until combined and set aside.
5. Add the olives, cucumber, tomatoes, feta cheese, parsley, and artichoke hearts (if using) to the orzo and toss well.
6. Shake the dressing once more and pour it over the salad, tossing to coat the ingredients. Serve.

Ingredient Tip: Cavender's All Purpose Greek Seasoning is the best! Use it on chicken breasts, legs, or thighs and pan sauté in olive oil for an easy dinner. It's also great for grilled vegetables, meatloaf, and burger meats.

Take a Shortcut: Many delicious ready-made Greek dressings are available. To save yourself a few minutes, you can use one of those instead of making the dressing.

Tortellini and Spinach Soup

IF MY FAMILY HAD TO VOTE on their favorite fast meal or soup, in unison we would all say it's this soup. It's a soup that doubles as a full meal, and we often just eat this for lunch or dinner. So much flavor develops so fast! I hope you love it as much as we do.

Serves: 4
Prep time: 5 minutes
Cook time: 15 minutes

2 tablespoons olive oil

6 garlic cloves, chopped

48 ounces chicken broth

Red pepper flakes (optional)

1 (16-ounce) package cheese tortellini

1 (14½-ounce) can crushed tomatoes

12 ounces fresh baby spinach

1. In a large pot over medium heat, heat the olive oil.
2. Add the garlic and sauté for no more than 45 seconds, taking care to not brown it.
3. Add the chicken broth and red pepper flakes (if using).
4. Increase the heat to high and bring the broth to a boil. When the broth is boiling, add the tortellini.
5. Halfway through the cooking time listed on the package, add the tomatoes, reduce the heat to medium-low, and continue cooking until the tortellini are tender.
6. Remove the pot from the heat and stir in the spinach. It will wilt in about a minute.
7. Taste the soup, adjust the seasoning if necessary, and serve.

Swap It: Make this a vegetarian dish by swapping the chicken broth for vegetable broth.

White Bean and Bacon Soup

YEARS AGO, AT A LUNCH WITH FRIENDS at Seasons 52, I ordered their white bean and bacon soup and became instantly smitten, so of course I had to replicate it. This hearty soup is perfect for crisp, cold days. It comes together quickly and reheats well. Drop Biscuits (page 59) are a wonderful accompaniment.

Serves: 4
Prep time: 10 minutes
Cook time: 20 minutes

6 bacon slices, chopped

½ cup diced onion

¼ cup diced carrots

3 garlic cloves, chopped

1 tablespoon olive oil or grapeseed oil (optional)

2 (15-ounce) cans cannellini beans, or other white beans, rinsed and drained

½ tablespoon dried basil

2 cups chicken stock

Pinch salt

Freshly ground black pepper

1. Heat a large pot over medium heat. Place the chopped bacon directly into the pot and cook, stirring periodically, until crisp.
2. Use a slotted spatula or spoon to transfer the bacon to a paper towel–lined plate. Set aside.
3. In the same pot, sauté the onion, carrots, and garlic in the bacon fat for 3 minutes. Add the garlic and sauté for another minute or two, stirring frequently. If the mixture becomes too dry, add the olive oil to finish cooking.
4. Add the beans, basil, and chicken stock, season with salt and black pepper, and stir well with a large spoon.
5. Reduce the heat to medium-low and simmer the soup for 12 to 15 minutes. With about 5 minutes left to go, use a potato masher or the back of a wooden spoon to mash some of the beans. This will add creaminess to the soup.
6. Ladle the soup into bowls, top with the bacon, and serve.

Swap It: Add cooked ground sausage to make this dish a full meal, or add chopped kale for greens. If you choose to add kale, do so just after you remove the bacon and before adding the onion, carrot, and garlic. You can also garnish the soup with shaved Parmesan cheese or a dollop of store-bought pesto.

Perfect Tomato Soup

NOT ONLY IS THIS TOMATO SOUP COMFORTING, it's also loaded with detoxifying ingredients. I often make this soup in a large quantity and enjoy it for three days for lunches and dinners when I want to eat light. The addition of pepitas gives me the crunch I look for in a meal to feel satisfied. Pair this soup with a Grown-Up Grilled Cheese sandwich (page 64) or Drop Biscuits (page 59) and make it a full meal.

Serves: 2 to 3
Prep time: 5 minutes
Cook time: 15 minutes

1 tablespoon olive oil

⅓ cup chopped Vidalia onion

1 tablespoon chopped fresh ginger

2 garlic cloves, minced

1 (28-ounce) can crushed fire-roasted tomatoes

1¼ cups vegetable stock, or chicken stock

1½ teaspoons salt

⅛ teaspoon freshly ground black pepper

1 tablespoon sugar

¼ cup torn fresh basil leaves (optional)

Pinch cayenne pepper (optional)

Optional garnishes: pepitas, shaved Parmesan cheese, chopped chives

1. In a medium pot over medium heat, heat the olive oil.
2. Add the onion and ginger, and sauté for 2 minutes, stirring frequently. Add the garlic and sauté for another 2 minutes.
3. Add the tomatoes, vegetable stock, salt, black pepper, and sugar and bring the mixture to a simmer for 5 minutes.
4. Add the basil leaves and cayenne (if using), taste, and adjust the seasonings if desired.
5. Garnish with any or all of the optional garnishes. Enjoy hot, at room temperature, or cold.

Ingredient Tip: To make this soup even faster, use garlic paste and ginger paste, found in tubes in the refrigerated produce section of most supermarkets, in place of the fresh garlic and ginger.

Swap It: Add in ½ cup of heavy (whipping) cream when you take the pot off the heat to make this a cream of tomato soup.

Egg Roll Bowl

THIS GENIUS IDEA, which started floating around on the internet a few years ago at the height of the "meal in a bowl" craze, comes together quickly. Any ground meat will work here, or even shrimp if you like. You will find yourself making this dish over and over again.

Serves: 4
Prep time: 10 minutes
Cook time: 15 minutes

---

1 tablespoon olive oil

1 pound ground chicken or pork

2 tablespoons sesame oil

¾ cup chopped Vidalia onion

2 garlic cloves, minced

1 tablespoon minced fresh ginger

1 tablespoon rice wine vinegar or white wine vinegar

5 tablespoons low-sodium soy sauce

1 (16-ounce bag) coleslaw mix

½ cup shredded or julienned carrots (if the coleslaw mix does not contain carrots)

3 scallions, thinly sliced or snipped, for garnish

1. Heat a large pan or skillet over medium-high heat. Pour in the olive oil and add the chicken or pork.
2. Cook, stirring often, until almost no pink remains in the chicken or pork. Use a slotted spatula or spoon to transfer the chicken or pork to a bowl. Drain the drippings into a sturdy container, such as a mug or bowl. Place in the refrigerator and, once hardened, scrape the drippings out and dispose of them in the garbage. (Draining fat into the sink can result in a blocked drain.)
3. Pour the sesame oil into the pan, still over medium-high heat. Once the oil begins to shimmer, add the onion and sauté, stirring regularly, for 2 minutes.
4. Add the garlic and ginger and sauté for 1 minute, then return the chicken or pork to the pan, stirring well to mix everything together.
5. Add the rice wine or white wine vinegar, soy sauce, coleslaw mix, and carrots (if using) and toss to combine.
6. Sauté for 5 to 6 minutes or until the slaw has wilted.
7. Remove from the heat, taste, and adjust the seasonings if necessary. Garnish with the scallions and serve.

Got Leftovers? This dish reheats nicely and is perfect for lunch, over rice, or even as a filling for lettuce wraps.

Swap It: Add 1 to 2 tablespoons of hoisin sauce for a depth of flavor. If you like things spicy, add a swirl of sriracha sauce. If you have packets of duck sauce or hot Chinese mustard from takeout lying around, squeeze some of it on top of the bowl as you would an egg roll.

Fajita Bowl

INSTEAD OF USING TRADITIONAL TORTILLAS, enjoy this fajita in a bowl. You can serve the fajitas over rice or over greens, like a salad. For the protein, choose steak, chicken, or shrimp. The beauty of this simple recipe is that you can enjoy it a multitude of ways . . . including as traditional fajitas *with* tortillas if you like.

Serves: 2
Prep time: 10 minutes
Cook time: 10 minutes

---

8 to 12 ounces steak, chicken, or shrimp

2 tablespoons fajita or taco seasoning, divided

2 tablespoons olive oil, divided

Freshly squeezed lime juice

1 large Vidalia onion, sliced

1 large green or red bell pepper, sliced

2 cups cooked white or brown rice, or salad greens

½ cup sliced tomatoes, or pico de gallo

½ cup canned black beans, drained and rinsed

1 avocado or ¾ cup premade guacamole

Optional toppings: sliced jalapeño pepper, chopped fresh cilantro, charred corn, sour cream, hot sauce

1. If using steak or chicken, slice it into strips about the width size of your pointer finger. If using shrimp, leave them whole but remove the tails and any bits of shell/legs. Season with 1 tablespoon (more or less, to taste) of fajita seasoning.
2. Heat a large skillet or sauté pan over high heat. Pour in 1 tablespoon of the olive oil. When it just begins to shimmer, add the meat/shrimp and sauté until done, 3 to 4 minutes. Spritz with lime juice during the last minute of cooking. Set aside.
3. Add the remaining 1 tablespoon of oil to the skillet, scrape up and remove any browned bits on the bottom of the skillet with a spatula, and add the onion and bell pepper. Season with the remaining 1 tablespoon of fajita seasoning (or to taste) and cook over medium-high heat until the vegetables are cooked, about 4 minutes.
4. Assemble the bowl by topping the rice with the meat/shrimp, onion-pepper mixture, tomatoes, beans, and guacamole. Garnish with any or all of the optional toppings and spritz with a little additional lime juice.

Ingredient Tip: Make your own fajita seasoning without any potential chemical additives. Simply combine 3 tablespoons of chili powder, 2 teaspoons of salt (or less if sodium is an issue), 2 teaspoons of ground cumin, 2 teaspoons of paprika, 2 teaspoons of dried oregano, 2 teaspoons of sugar, 1 teaspoon of garlic powder, 1 teaspoon of onion powder, and ½ teaspoon of red pepper flakes or cayenne pepper. Whisk in a bowl or shake in a bag until fully combined. These quantities will make just under ½ cup of seasoning.

Quinoa Crunch Bowl

A CRUNCHY TEXTURE can often make a meal feel extra satisfying. Between the crisp vegetables and the quinoa (or grain of choice), this simple dish satisfies. If you like, add some shredded chicken or 1-inch pieces of firm, pan-seared tofu for a protein hit.

Serves: 2
Prep time: 10 minutes
Cook time: 15 minutes

1½ cups cooked quinoa

Salt

Freshly ground black pepper

2 cups shelled edamame

2 cups shredded carrot

1 cup chopped cucumber

½ cup chopped red onion

2 tablespoons chopped fresh cilantro

1 jalapeño pepper, seeded and sliced (optional)

Store-bought sesame ginger vinaigrette or Asian flavored dressing

Optional toppings: chopped radishes, chopped peanuts, raw shredded red cabbage

1. Season the quinoa with salt and black pepper and divide between 2 serving bowls.
2. In a mixing bowl, combine the edamame, carrot, cucumber, red onion, cilantro, and jalapeño pepper (if using).
3. Add the dressing and toss to coat the vegetables; season with a bit more black pepper and spoon the mixture atop the quinoa. Garnish with any or all of the optional toppings.

Shopping Tip: In addition to frozen edamame in the shell, you can typically find already shelled edamame in both the freezer section and the produce section.

Swap It: You can swap the quinoa for brown rice, farro, or your favorite grain.

6

Meatless Mains

Goat Cheese–Stuffed Tomatoes

BITE AFTER BITE, something about the combination of flavors and textures of these stuffed tomatoes keeps you coming back for more. Try serving them over a bed of arugula or microgreens, drizzled with oil and a spritz of fresh lemon. These also work well as mini appetizers.

Serves: 2
Prep time: 10 minutes
Cook time: 10 minutes

4 medium tomatoes

Salt

Freshly ground black pepper

1 cup panko bread crumbs

6 fresh basil leaves, cut into ribbons

1 garlic clove, minced

2 tablespoons olive oil

16 ounces garlic and herb goat cheese

1. Turn the oven's broiler to high.
2. Cut a circle into the top of each tomato and gently remove the top. Then, using a melon baller, serrated spoon, or knife, gently remove the core and pulp of the tomato. Be careful to not break through the skin.
3. Season the inside of the tomatoes with salt and black pepper, then flip them over onto a paper towel for 5 minutes to drain.
4. In a small bowl, combine the panko, basil, and garlic. Season with salt and black pepper, drizzle with the olive oil, and mix well. Set aside.
5. To stuff the tomatoes, fill them three-quarters full with goat cheese. Top with the panko mixture, place on a baking sheet, and broil for 5 to 8 minutes or until the bread crumbs are golden brown and the tomatoes are wilted.

Swap It: You can also chop up olives, roasted red peppers, or artichokes to mix in with the cheese.

Avocado Caprese

YEARS AGO, WHEN I POSTED THIS RECIPE on my website, I almost broke Facebook! Seriously though, for whatever reason, it was viewed by millions of people. All the components of this dish work together in harmony and look beautiful when plated. I highly recommend a drizzle of balsamic glaze to bring all the flavors together.

Serves: 4
Prep time: 10 minutes

½ cup grapeseed oil or olive oil

4 garlic cloves, minced

Kosher salt

Freshly ground black pepper

2 avocados

1 pint grape tomatoes, halved

16 bocconcini (small mozzarella balls), halved

Chopped fresh basil leaves, for garnish

Balsamic glaze, for garnish (optional)

1. In a small bowl or mason jar, combine the grapeseed oil, garlic, salt, and black pepper. Be liberal with the salt and pepper. Shake or mix well and allow the flavors to mingle while you prepare the rest of the recipe.
2. With a sharp knife, cut the avocados lengthwise all the way around the pit, then twist apart the two halves. To remove the pit, gently hit it with the sharp edge of the knife, just enough so the knife catches, then twist the pit out of the avocado and discard it.
3. Season the avocado halves with a bit of salt and pepper, then drag a fork across the top of each half, like you would use a rake on soil, and dig up the avocado flesh a bit. Set aside.
4. In a small bowl, toss the tomatoes, bocconcini, and basil together with a spoonful of the garlic-oil mixture. Spoon the mixture over the avocados, drizzle with balsamic glaze (if using), and dig in.

Got Leftovers? If you have leftover garlic oil, use it as a quick marinade for steaks, whole fish fillets, or shrimp.

Ingredient Tip: Balsamic glaze is readily available in most grocery stores, typically in the same aisle as salad dressing or by the Italian specialty goods. It keeps well in the refrigerator. I regularly use it for light tomato and mozzarella salads for lunch.

Pasta Puttanesca

THIS IS ONE OF THE MOST FLAVORFUL PASTA SAUCES I know. Puttanesca traditionally contains anchovies that lend a salty, briny flavor to the sauce, but here the dish is made vegetarian by replacing the anchovies with Kalamata olives and a bit of their liquid.

Serves: 2
Prep time: 10 minutes
Cook time: 10 minutes

3 tablespoons olive oil

2 large garlic cloves, minced

½ teaspoon red pepper flakes

1 (28-ounce) can whole peeled Italian tomatoes, with their juice

¾ cup Kalamata olives, pitted and chopped, plus 2 tablespoons of their juice

¼ cup capers, rinsed and drained

1 teaspoon sugar

Salt

Freshly ground black pepper

¼ cup chopped fresh parsley

12 ounces spaghetti or linguine pasta

Parmesan cheese, freshly grated, for garnish

1. Heat a medium pot over medium heat. Pour the olive oil into the pot and when it begins to shimmer, add the garlic and sauté for 60 seconds, stirring the whole time.
2. Add the red pepper flakes and tomatoes and their juice. Use a potato masher or the back of a wooden spoon to break up the tomatoes a bit.
3. Add the olives and their juice, capers, and sugar and stir until fully combined. Season with salt and black pepper to taste.
4. Lower the heat and allow the sauce to simmer for 7 to 8 minutes until thickened, then remove the pot from the heat.
5. Taste and adjust the seasoning to your liking.
6. While the sauce simmers, bring a large pot of salted water to a rolling boil, add the pasta, and cook for 6 to 7 minutes, stirring with a wooden spoon or tongs so the noodles don't stick together. Remove from the heat and carefully drain the pasta in a colander.
7. Add the drained pasta to the pot of sauce, add the parsley, toss to coat, and plate.
8. Top with Parmesan cheese.

Zucchini Cakes

THESE ZUCCHINI CAKES are one of my favorite side dishes (that could also double as a light lunch) and one of the most delicious ways I have found to enjoy zucchini. Even the kids love them, and that's a big win in my world. You can make these as mini cakes for a vegetarian appetizer offering.

Makes: 4 cakes
Prep time: 10 minutes
Cook time: 10 minutes

1 large zucchini

½ cup plain panko
    bread crumbs

½ cup shredded
    Parmesan cheese

¼ cup chopped scallions

Pinch kosher salt

Pinch freshly ground
    black pepper

1 egg, plus 1 egg yolk

Grapeseed or olive oil

1. Grate the zucchini and squeeze out as much liquid as you can. Blot with paper towels to dry it further.
2. In a medium bowl, combine the zucchini, panko, Parmesan cheese, scallions, salt, and black pepper. Toss until combined.
3. Crack the egg into a bowl. Add the yolk (see Ingredient Tip). Beat the yolk and egg together with a fork.
4. Add the egg mixture to the zucchini mixture and toss with a fork until combined.
5. Shape the mixture into 4 cakes, pressing firmly, like making a snowball.
6. Heat a large frying pan or skillet over medium-high heat. Pour in just enough oil to coat the bottom of the pan, and when the oil begins to shimmer, add the cakes and cook them for 2 to 3 minutes per side, flipping gently, or until golden brown on both sides.

Ingredient Tip: To separate an egg, crack the egg and pass the yolk back and forth between the two halves of the eggshell until you've isolated the yolk as much as possible (do this over a different bowl to catch the unneeded egg white, which you can discard).

Grilled Peach and Ricotta Flatbread

WHIPPED RICOTTA IS A MAGICAL INGREDIENT to be enjoyed with sweet or savory toppings. It's wonderful in this flatbread topped with grilled peaches, fresh thyme, and honey. Use this recipe as a base for your creativity; swap out the peaches for roasted strawberries and arugula, or pan-sautéed figs and walnuts, or roasted tomatoes with a drizzle of balsamic. Top this flatbread any way you like!

Serves: 4
Prep time: 10 minutes
Cook time: 5 minutes

1 (8- to 10-inch) naan or 4 smaller flatbreads

1 to 2 teaspoons olive oil

16 ounces full-fat ricotta

Grilled Peaches (page 144), chopped

1 teaspoon chopped fresh thyme leaves

2 tablespoons honey

1. Preheat the oven to 350ºF.
2. Brush the top side of the naan with the olive oil and place it on a baking sheet.
3. Bake the naan for 4 to 5 minutes.
4. While the naan is baking, put the ricotta in a stand mixer or use a hand mixer and whip for 3 minutes.
5. Top the warm flatbread(s)with the whipped ricotta, peaches, thyme, and honey.

Avocado Pasta

IF YOU HAVE NEVER USED AVOCADOS as a base for pasta sauce, all I can say is what took you so long? This is a flavor combination you will want to enjoy again soon. If you want to make this dish with a protein, try adding some shredded chicken (from a store-bought rotisserie chicken) to the sauce or crumble cooked bacon over the top.

Serves: 3
Prep time: 10 minutes
Cook time: 10 minutes

2 avocados

¾ tablespoon salt

¾ pound linguini

3 garlic cloves

1 jalapeño pepper, halved, seeds and stem removed

⅓ cup fresh basil leaves

Juice of 1 lemon

¼ cup olive oil

Freshly ground black pepper

Chopped fresh basil, for garnish

Parmesan cheese, grated, for garnish, or Asiago or Pecorino Romano

Red pepper flakes (optional)

1. With a sharp knife, cut the avocado lengthwise all the way around the pit, then twist apart the two halves. To remove the pit, gently hit it with the sharp edge of the knife, just enough so the knife catches, then twist the pit out of the avocado and discard it.
2. Fill a large pot with water, add the salt, and bring to a rolling boil over high heat. Add the linguini and cook for 6 to 7 minutes, stirring with a wooden spoon or tongs so the noodles don't stick together. Remove the pot from the heat and carefully reserve about ½ cup of the pasta cooking water. Drain the pasta in a colander and set aside.
3. While the pasta is cooking, in a food processor or high-powered blender, pulse the garlic, jalapeño pepper, basil, avocados, and lemon juice until almost smooth.
4. Drizzle in the olive oil and pulse until smooth.
5. Gradually add the reserved pasta water until the sauce reaches the consistency you enjoy.
6. Season with salt and black pepper, pulse to combine, taste, and adjust the seasoning if necessary.
7. Toss the sauce and pasta together until evenly coated, portion out the pasta, and garnish with Parmesan cheese and red pepper flakes (if using).

Homemade Veggie Burgers

FORGET THE HYPE ABOUT LAB-CREATED MEATLESS BURGERS and go with one that you can make yourself with everyday ingredients. These burgers are full of flavor and texture and are a great alternative when you're looking for a meatless meal or need a dish for vegetarians at a barbecue. Serve the burgers plain with a side of roasted veggies or on a toasted bun with sriracha mayo and your favorite burger toppings.

Serves: 4
Prep time: 10 minutes
Cook time: 15 minutes

1 (14-ounce) can black beans, rinsed and drained

1 egg, plus 1 egg yolk

⅓ cup chopped Vidalia onion

1 cup chopped unpeeled zucchini

2 garlic cloves, minced, or 3 tablespoons garlic paste

1½ cups cooked rice

½ cup shredded Parmesan cheese

Pinch salt

Pinch freshly ground black pepper

½ cup panko bread crumbs

1 tablespoon olive oil

⅓ cup mayonnaise

½ tablespoon sriracha, or more to taste

1. In a mixing bowl, mash the beans a bit with a potato masher (about 4 mashes should do it; you still want some whole or partially whole beans).
2. Crack the egg into a bowl. Add the yolk and beat them together with a fork. (See the tip on page 83 for how to separate eggs.)
3. Add the onion, zucchini, garlic, rice, Parmesan cheese, egg mixture, salt, and black pepper to the bowl and mix well.
4. Sprinkle in the panko and mix until combined.
5. Place the mixture in the freezer to chill for 10 minutes, then form it into patties, pressing down firmly to shape them. If they do not hold their shape, add a little more panko.
6. Heat a nonstick pan over medium heat. Pour in the olive oil and tilt the pan to evenly coat the bottom in a very thin layer.
7. Once the oil begins to shimmer, gently add the burgers, making sure not to crowd them. Cook for 2 to 2½ minutes per side, flipping them gently, until each side has a nice golden-brown crust.
8. In a small bowl, stir together the mayonnaise and sriracha and use to top the burgers.

Pro Tip: Making this mixture the day before (or morning of) you plan on cooking the burgers will deepen their flavor. Make the mixture and form into patties, cover, and cook when ready.

Artichoke Française

OUR FAMILY LOVES THIS DISH. As a matter of fact, it's been my daughter and nieces' "signature dish" since they were eight years old. When we have it, they make it. Enjoy this dish by itself, over rice, or over pasta. The sauce easily doubles if you like your artichokes saucier.

Serves: 4
Prep time: 10 minutes
Cook time: 10 minutes

2 (14-ounce) cans whole artichoke hearts, drained and halved

¾ cup all-purpose flour

Salt

Freshly ground black pepper

2 large eggs, beaten

2 tablespoons grated Parmesan cheese, plus more for garnish (optional)

2 tablespoons minced fresh parsley, divided

3 to 4 tablespoons olive oil

¼ cup dry white wine

2 tablespoons butter

Juice of 1 lemon

1. Drain the artichoke hearts in a colander. Gently pat them dry with paper towels.
2. Put the flour in a bowl and season it with salt and black pepper (if you enjoy heat, sprinkle in a little cayenne pepper).
3. In another small bowl, whisk together the eggs, Parmesan cheese, ½ tablespoon of parsley, and a pinch of salt and black pepper.
4. Coat the artichokes in the flour, tap off any excess, and then dip them into the egg mixture.
5. Pour just enough olive oil into a large sauté pan to coat the bottom, then 1 more tablespoon on top of that.
6. Heat the oil over medium-high heat. When it begins to shimmer, add the artichokes and pan-fry them, gently flipping once with tongs or a small spatula, until they are crispy and golden brown on both sides. You will need to cook them in batches, adding more oil when necessary.
7. Transfer the cooked artichokes to a paper towel–lined plate. Set aside.
8. Deglaze the pan by adding the white wine. Allow it to simmer for a minute over medium-low heat, then add the butter and lemon juice. Whisk everything together and let it thicken for a minute (any residual panko from the artichokes will help the sauce thicken). Add ½ tablespoon of parsley and season with salt and black pepper.
9. Place the artichokes on a plate, pour over the sauce, sprinkle with the remaining 1 tablespoon of parsley and grated Parmesan cheese (if using).

Vegetable Frittata

IF YOU ENJOY ZUCCHINI, you will find this frittata irresistible. The vegetables, eggs, and cheese complement each another deliciously, resulting in a light meal perfect for breakfast, lunch, brunch, or dinner. Once you know how to make a frittata, you can customize them any way you like using seasonal ingredients or whatever you have on hand.

Serves: 4
Prep time: 10 minutes
Cook time: 15 minutes

1 pound unpeeled zucchini, thinly sliced

1 teaspoon salt

5 large eggs

¼ cup chopped onion

½ teaspoon oregano (fresh or dried)

1 tablespoon chopped fresh parsley

3 to 4 tablespoons chopped red, yellow, or orange bell pepper

½ cup shredded Monterey Jack, Parmesan, or Cheddar cheese

Pinch salt

Freshly ground black pepper

1½ tablespoons olive oil

1. Put the zucchini in a colander, sprinkle with the salt, toss, and let drain while you prepare the other ingredients.
2. In a small bowl, whisk the eggs until fully combined. Set aside.
3. Blot the zucchini as dry as you can with paper towels, then transfer it to a bowl. Add the onion, oregano, parsley, bell pepper, cheese, salt, and black pepper.
4. Turn the oven's broiler to high. Place the rack in the middle of the oven.
5. Heat a 10-inch oven-safe skillet over medium-high heat. Pour in the olive oil, then add the zucchini mixture and cook until the zucchini is just tender, about 5 minutes.
6. Reduce the heat to low.
7. Give the eggs a quick whisk again and pour them over the zucchini mixture.
8. Cook until the edges of the frittata have set and the center has begun to set, 4 to 5 minutes.
9. Broil the frittata 3 to 4 minutes until it is set, then remove it from the oven and serve.

Swap It: Use feta cheese instead of other cheese suggestions. If you enjoy tomatoes on your eggs, top the frittata with pico de gallo or salsa.

Veggie Burritos

MY FRIEND AND FELLOW COOKBOOK AUTHOR Lisa Grant makes these meatless burritos loaded with mushrooms. Top with salsa and guacamole and you have yourself a hearty meatless meal.

Serves: 2
Prep time: 5 minutes
Cook time: 20 minutes

---

2 tablespoons olive oil

¼ cup finely diced onion

1 pound button or shiitake mushrooms, sliced

1½ teaspoons chili powder

1 tablespoon tomato paste

2 burrito tortillas, or taco shells

½ cup shredded Mexican cheese blend

½ cup guacamole, homemade or store-bought

½ cup salsa

1. Preheat the oven to 350°F.
2. In a large pan, heat the olive oil over medium heat. When it begins to shimmer, add the onion and sauté for 3 to 4 minutes or until it starts to turn translucent.
3. Add the mushrooms and cook for 6 to 7 minutes or until soft, stirring often.
4. Drain the liquid from the pan.
5. Add the chili powder and tomato paste to the pan. Stir to incorporate and cook for 2 minutes more.
6. Divide the mixture between the tortillas.
7. Sprinkle with the cheese, then roll up each burrito in aluminum foil and bake for 6 to 7 minutes, just until the cheese melts.
8. Top with the guacamole and salsa and dig in with a fork and knife.

Butternut Squash Rigatoni

SWEET BUTTERNUT SQUASH IS WONDERFUL in this pasta dish. Adding a little maple syrup helps caramelize the squash, but if sweet is not your thing or you are watching your sugar intake, you can easily omit the syrup without sacrificing any flavor. Look for pre-cut butternut squash in your produce area to save time and hassle.

Serves: 2
Prep time: 5 minutes
Cook time: 20 minutes

8 ounces rigatoni pasta

2 tablespoons olive oil

2 garlic cloves, minced

1½ cups peeled and cubed butternut squash

Salt

1 tablespoon maple syrup

3 tablespoons butter

4 fresh sage leaves

Freshly ground black pepper

⅓ cup grated Parmesan cheese

1. Cook the pasta according to the package instructions until al dente, meaning it is still slightly chewy and firm to the bite.
2. While the pasta is cooking, in a large nonstick skillet over medium heat, heat the olive oil. When the oil begins to shimmer, add the garlic and sauté, stirring frequently, for 1 to 2 minutes or until fragrant but not brown.
3. Add the butternut squash and season with salt. Scoop out 2 tablespoons of the pasta water and add it to the skillet.
4. Cover the skillet and allow the squash to cook for 8 to 10 minutes, stirring occasionally.
5. With 2 minutes cooking time to go, add the maple syrup, butter, and sage leaves. Gently stir. The squash should be tender and the butter beginning to brown.
6. Drain the pasta, reserving 2 to 3 tablespoons of the cooking water. Add the water to the skillet and then pour the skillet contents over the pasta.
7. Season with salt and black pepper, toss, sprinkle with the Parmesan cheese, and serve.

Swap It: You could serve this sauce and squash over cheese ravioli in place of the rigatoni. You can swap out the rigatoni for penne or rotelle pasta as well.

Brussels Sprouts and Walnuts

MY WHOLE FAMILY LOVES BRUSSELS SPROUTS. It took years for me to like them because my parents (sorry, Mom and Dad) boiled them to death. Once I realized what heat in a pan or oven could do to sprouts, I have loved their natural nutty flavor and crisp texture. My daughter has been cooking Brussels sprouts for herself since she was seven; they are her favorite food.

Serves: 2
Prep time: 10 minutes
Cook time: 15 minutes

---

1 cup walnut or pecan pieces

1½ tablespoons olive oil

1 pound Brussels sprouts

Salt

Freshly ground black pepper

¼ teaspoon smoky paprika

½ cup pomegranate seeds

½ cup crumbled goat cheese or feta cheese (optional)

1. In a large skillet or frying pan, toast the walnuts over medium-high heat, moving them around almost constantly for 3 to 4 minutes. Be careful not to burn them. There is no need to add oil, because nuts naturally contain oil. When cooked, transfer them to a bowl and set aside.
2. On a cutting board, cut off the bottoms of the Brussels sprouts and pull off any leaves that have dark spots or have yellowed.
3. Cut the sprouts into halves or quarters depending on their size.
4. Replace the skillet over medium-high heat and pour in the olive oil, then add the sprouts. Cook them, moving them around often for about 10 minutes or until cooked to your liking. Season them with salt, black pepper, and paprika along the way. Brussels sprouts need a decent amount of salt.
5. Add some extra oil if necessary, and once they are cooked , remove the skillet from the heat, add the walnuts, and toss, seasoning with additional salt and pepper if necessary.
6. Slide the Brussels sprouts into a serving bowl, sprinkle with the pomegranate seeds, and top with the goat cheese.

Ingredient Tip: If you enjoy balsamic glaze and have some on hand, a drizzle of that on top of the sprouts is lovely. You can also oven roast the sprouts at 400°F, pulling them out of the oven from time to time to toss them.

Swap It: If you eat bacon, start this dish off by chopping 6 bacon slices and cooking them in the skillet. Remove the bacon when crisp and add the sprouts, using the bacon fat in place of the oil.

Asparagus Noodle Bowl

THIS BRIGHT VEGETABLE NOODLE BOWL makes for a healthy and light meal. It's a nice change from the typical zucchini noodle. Pair this bowl with warm biscuits or a loaf of crusty bread and butter. I enjoy using basil pesto, which you can easily find in the grocery store with the other jarred pasta sauces.

Serves: 2 to 3
Prep time: 10 minutes
Cook time: 5 minutes

1½ pounds asparagus (not thin asparagus)

1½ teaspoons olive oil

Salt

Freshly ground black pepper

1 teaspoon freshly squeezed lemon juice

⅓ cup basil pesto

⅓ cup crumbled feta cheese

Red pepper flakes (optional)

¼ cup pine nuts (optional)

1. Cut just the top tips off the asparagus spears and set them aside.
2. Using a vegetable peeler, start from just above the bottom of each asparagus spear and run the peeler up firmly, shaving each spear into strips. Toss the very bottom nub of what's left of the asparagus away.
3. Heat a sauté pan over medium-high heat. Pour the olive oil into the pan, and when the oil begins to shimmer, add the asparagus noodles. Season with a little salt and black pepper and sauté the noodles, moving them around with a spoon just until they brighten up, 90 seconds to 2 minutes.
4. Spritz with the lemon juice and stir in the pesto.
5. Remove from the heat and add the feta, red pepper flakes, and pine nuts (if using).

Parmesan Baked Zucchini and Tomatoes

MY UNCLE ROY, WHO WAS PASSIONATE about eating organic way before it was a thing, introduced me to this dish years ago. I loved how he overlapped the tomatoes and zucchini, like a ratatouille, yet simpler. I use plum tomatoes for this because they're closer in size to the zucchini; however, you can choose grape tomatoes, which make the dish quicker to prepare because you don't need to slice them.

Serves: 4
Prep time: 10 minutes
Cook time: 20 minutes

Nonstick cooking spray

2 zucchini, unpeeled

6 to 8 plum tomatoes (depends on their size)

Salt

Freshly ground black pepper

2 tablespoons olive oil

1½ tablespoons garlic paste or 1 teaspoon garlic powder

¾ cup freshly shredded Parmesan or Asiago cheese

1. Preheat the oven to 425ºF.
2. Spray a casserole dish lightly with cooking spray.
3. Slice the zucchini and the tomatoes each to ½ inch thick and season them with salt and black pepper.
4. In a small bowl or mason jar, combine the olive oil and garlic paste and whisk or shake to combine.
5. Place the zucchini and tomato slices in the prepared casserole dish, overlapping them a bit row after row, drizzle with the garlic oil, and place in the oven.
6. Lower the oven temperature to 400ºF and bake for 15 minutes.
7. Pull the dish out, sprinkle with the Parmesan cheese and bake for another 5 minutes.

Pro Tip: As much as I adore fresh garlic, it will burn in a hot oven, so garlic paste is the way to go here. That or garlic powder. If you have time, you can also infuse the oil with fresh garlic. Simply combine ¼ cup of olive oil, 2 tablespoons of chopped garlic, and a hefty pinch of salt and black pepper. Let it sit on the counter for 20 to 30 minutes, stirring every so often. Strain it, and that's it.

Swap It: You can use 1 green zucchini and 1 yellow squash for more color if you like.

7

Seafood

Garlic Shrimp

TREAT YOURSELF OR IMPRESS GUESTS with little effort with this simple yet flavorful dish that is also delicious served over pasta. Serve with a warm crusty bread (to sop up the sauce) and a salad, and you have yourself an easy restaurant-quality meal at home.

Serves: 4
Prep time: 15 minutes
Cook time: 10 minutes

3 tablespoons olive oil

10 garlic cloves, chopped

1½ pounds raw large shrimp, peeled, cleaned, tails removed

Kosher salt

Freshly ground black pepper

8 tablespoons (1 stick) butter, cut into 6 chunks, divided

⅓ cup freshly squeezed lemon juice

3 to 4 tablespoons capers, plus a splash of their juice

Cayenne pepper (optional)

2 tablespoons chopped parsley

1. In a large pan, heat the olive oil over medium-high heat.
2. When the oil begins to shimmer, add the garlic and sauté for 30 seconds.
3. Add the shrimp and sauté for 1 to 2 minutes, then lower the heat to medium, sprinkle with a pinch of salt and black pepper, add half the butter and the lemon juice, and continue to sauté until cooked through (2 to 3 more minutes), turning the shrimp occasionally to ensure they cook evenly.
4. Remove the pan from the heat, add the capers and a splash of their juice, sprinkle with the cayenne (if using), parsley, and the remaining butter.
5. Toss until the butter is melted and serve immediately.

Shopping Tip: If you find cleaned raw shrimp in the grocery store, the prep time is cut in half.

Blackened Tuna

BLACKENED TUNA DOESN'T NEED TO BE A DISH you can only enjoy at a restaurant; it's incredibly easy to make at home and makes for a fantastic, super fast, and flavorful dinner. Enjoy it sliced atop a salad for lunch or sliced and served with wasabi or a dipping sauce as an appetizer. You can also use this same method with salmon or grouper.

Serves: 2
Prep time: 5 minutes
Cook time: 5 minutes

---

2 (½- to ¾-pound) fresh, good quality tuna steaks

2 tablespoons olive oil, plus more if necessary

3 tablespoons blackening seasoning

1 lemon, cut into quarters

1. Coat each piece of tuna with the olive oil, rubbing it all over with your fingertips.
2. Place the blackening seasoning on a plate, then dip and press each piece of tuna into the seasoning, coating it evenly. Add more seasoning to the plate if needed.
3. Heat a large cast iron skillet or frying pan over high heat until the pan is very hot, then carefully place the tuna steaks in the pan. Make sure not to crowd the steaks.
4. Cook for about 2 minutes per side for medium rare (depending on the size and thickness of the tuna). When you flip the tuna, you may need to add a drizzle of oil.
5. Remove the tuna from the pan with a spatula and plate it.
6. Serve with a lemon quarter and enjoy.

Pro Tip: For the freshest tuna, look for tuna that looks moist and bright.

Shopping Tip: Look for blackening seasoning near the seafood case or in the spice area of the baking section. The best I have found is Paul Prudhomme's Blackened Redfish Magic or Blackened Seasoning Blend.

Salmon Burgers

FOR THOSE WHO EAT SALMON a couple times a week, these salmon burgers are a flavorful way to switch things up. These are also a fantastic alternative to traditional burgers. If you have leftover salmon, even if it's glazed or seasoned, you can flake it and use it for these burgers.

Serves: 3 to 4
Prep time: 10 minutes
Cook time: 20 minutes

¾ pound salmon fillet

Salt

Freshly ground black pepper

¼ cup thinly sliced scallions

2 tablespoons chopped flat-leaf parsley

¾ cup fresh bread crumbs from a loaf of French bread

2 tablespoons mayonnaise

Freshly squeezed lemon juice

1 tablespoon coarse Dijon mustard (such as Grey Poupon Country Dijon)

Olive oil

Your favorite hamburger buns, such as Hawaiian, potato, or Kaiser

Optional toppings: tartar sauce, mayonnaise, lettuce, sliced tomato

1. Fill a medium saucepan with water about ¾ inch deep. Put the pan over high heat and bring the water to a boil, then reduce the heat to a simmer.
2. Season the salmon with salt and black pepper.
3. Place the salmon in the pan, cover, and cook for 8 to 10 minutes until just cooked through (the cook time depends on the thickness of the salmon).
4. Remove the salmon from the pan and gently flake it into a bowl. If it has skin on one side, just work the meat away from the skin. You can also cool the fish and refrigerate it at this point for use the next day.
5. Add the scallions, parsley, bread crumbs, mayonnaise, lemon juice, and mustard to the bowl with the salmon. Season with salt and black pepper and gently combine the mixture with your hands. Don't overwork it.
6. Form the mixture into burgers and place them on a plate lined with parchment or wax paper.
7. Return the skillet to medium heat and pour in just enough olive oil to lightly coat the bottom. Add the burgers (allowing room between each cake to flip them) and cook for 3 to 4 minutes per side, adding a little more oil if necessary. If the burgers begin to brown too much, remove the skillet from the heat for 15 to 30 seconds and reduce the heat to low to finish them off.
8. Place the salmon burgers on rolls and enjoy plain or with some of the optional toppings.

Pro Tip: These burgers can be made a day ahead and kept wrapped in the refrigerator.

Swap It: Skip the bun and enjoy these alongside a side vegetable or two. To make a quick remoulade to enjoy on the burger, combine mayonnaise with a squeeze of fresh lemon, a spoonful or pickle relish, and a sprinkle of black pepper.

Spicy Shrimp Ramen Noodle Soup

CHANGE UP THE WAY YOU ENJOY a packet of ramen noodles by creating your own broth and adding some shrimp. If spicy is not your thing, swap out the chili with garlic sauce and use garlic instead. You can always make the base of this soup ahead of time, then add the noodles when you're ready to enjoy.

Serves: 2
Prep time: 10 minutes
Cook time: 10 minutes

1 tablespoon olive oil

½ cup sliced button or baby portabella mushrooms

¼ cup thinly sliced carrots

4 cups chicken or vegetable stock

1 teaspoon grated fresh ginger

2 tablespoons soy sauce

1 to 2 tablespoons chili with garlic sauce

12 medium raw shrimp, peeled, cleaned, and tails removed

2 (3-ounce) packages plain ramen noodles

Juice of ½ lime

2 scallions, thinly sliced

Chopped fresh cilantro or chopped fresh Thai basil, for garnish (optional)

1. In a medium pot over medium heat, heat the olive oil until it shimmers. Add the mushrooms and carrots and sauté for 4 minutes.
2. Add the stock, ginger, soy sauce, chili with garlic sauce, and bring to a boil.
3. Add the shrimp and noodles (discard the seasoning packs) and boil for 3 to 4 minutes or until the shrimp turns pink and the noodles are cooked.
4. Remove the pot from the heat, taste, and adjust the seasoning if necessary.
5. Spoon into bowls (6 shrimp in each bowl), add a squeeze of lime juice, garnish with scallions and cilantro (if using), and enjoy.

Swap It: If you choose to not use chili with garlic sauce, replace that with 2 minced garlic cloves. Add the garlic halfway through sautéing the carrots and mushrooms.

Crab Cakes

I HAVE BEEN MAKING THESE CRAB CAKES for over half my life. Just about everyone who has had one (or three) said they're the best they've had . . . ever! If you're looking to impress or looking for an amazing meal for half the cost of going out, this is it! Serve with steamed green beans tossed in butter and seasoned with salt and black pepper. The suggested quick remoulade is fantastic with the crab cakes.

Serves: 4
Prep time: 10 minutes
Cook time: 5 minutes

1 (1-pound) can jumbo lump crabmeat

1 fresh French baguette

4 scallions, thinly sliced, both green and white parts

½ tablespoon freshly grated lemon zest

½ tablespoon freshly squeezed lemon juice

6 to 8 tablespoons mayonnaise

Pinch cayenne pepper

Olive oil

Remoulade

1 cup mayonnaise

1 teaspoon freshly squeezed lemon juice

1 teaspoon Worcestershire sauce

2 tablespoons sweet relish (not the type with mustard)

Pinch cayenne pepper

1. Drain the excess liquid from the can of crabmeat and place the crabmeat in a mixing bowl.
2. Dig out the insides from the baguette, crumble it into 1¼ cups of bread crumbs and add them to the bowl.
3. Add the scallions, lemon zest, lemon juice, mayonnaise, and cayenne and, with your hands, gently mix it until it's incorporated. Try to not break up all the lumps of crabmeat too much.
4. With your hands, form the mixture into about 7 crab cakes.
5. Pop the crab cakes in the freezer for 10 minutes or, if you're making them ahead of time, place them in the refrigerator, covered, for up to 24 hours.
6. When you're ready to cook, heat a nonstick frying pan or skillet over medium-high heat, and add just enough olive oil to coat the surface. When the oil begins to shimmer, add the cakes. Make sure to allow enough room between cakes for easy flipping.
7. Turn the heat down to medium and cook for 2 minutes or so per side, just until they have crisped up and formed a nice crust. Never press down on a crab cake while it cooks.
8. Remove from the pan and serve with the remoulade sauce.

FOR THE REMOULADE

Combine all the ingredients in a bowl and stir until fully blended. Taste and adjust for the level of spiciness you enjoy.

Ingredient Tip: The remoulade sauce is delicious with these crab cakes, but if you happen to find Cajun remoulade at the market, you can purchase that instead of making it.

Halibut in Thai Curry Sauce

THIS IS A RESTAURANT-QUALITY DISH that you can make in 30 minutes. But don't tell anyone how easy it was to make; just sit back and soak up the praise! Serve some sautéed spinach and rice alongside. Jasmine rice works well, or try a subtle coconut rice, which is delicious with this dish.

Serves: 4
Prep time: 5 minutes
Cook time: 25 minutes

4 (4-ounce) pieces
  fresh halibut

½ teaspoon salt, plus more
  for seasoning the sauce

½ teaspoon freshly ground
  black pepper, plus more
  for seasoning the sauce

½ teaspoon paprika

3 garlic cloves, minced

1 tablespoon minced
  fresh ginger

⅓ Vidalia onion, cut
  into chunks

3 tablespoons lime juice

3 tablespoons olive oil, plus
  more if necessary

2 tablespoons chopped
  fresh parsley

2 to 3 tablespoons Thai red
  curry paste

3 tablespoons tomato paste

¾ cup dry white wine

1 cup unsweetened
  coconut milk

Pinch cayenne pepper
  (optional)

1. Season the halibut with the salt, pepper, and paprika. Set aside.
2. In a bowl, combine the garlic, ginger, onion, and lime juice. Set aside.
3. Heat the olive oil in a nonstick skillet or frying pan over medium-high heat until it just begins to shimmer. Add the halibut and sear for 2 to 3 minutes per side until a golden-brown crust forms and the fish is cooked through. (The cook time will vary based on the thickness of the fish.)
4. Carefully transfer the fish to a baking sheet or plate tented with aluminum foil and set aside.
5. In the same skillet, sauté the garlic, ginger, onion, and lime mixture for 4 minutes. If needed, add a smidge more.
6. Add the Thai red curry paste and tomato paste; blend well with a small whisk or spatula and sauté for 3 minutes.
7. Add the wine and stir vigorously. Once the sauce is simmering, add the coconut milk and season to taste with salt and black pepper. If you like spice, add a pinch or two of cayenne pepper.
8. Simmer the sauce for 10 minutes, then remove from the heat.
9. Place the fish gently into the pan of sauce, allow it to sit for a minute or two, garnish with the chopped parsley, and serve.

Ingredient Tip: Some coconut milk may look like it's solidified; that's okay, because it will melt as you use it.

Shopping Tip: For both the coconut milk and Thai red curry paste, I like the brand THAI. Look for it in the Asian section at your grocery store.

Swap It: Swap the olive oil for butter; it will make a slightly richer and more flavorful sauce.

Asian Salmon in Foil

FOR MORE THAN HALF OF MY LIFE, I wouldn't even taste salmon, even though I love fish and most seafood. I was convinced I didn't like it. Boy, was I wrong. This dish is a great introduction to salmon for anyone who may feel the same as I once did. This is one of those dinners you will find yourself making again and again. It is delicious with steamed rice or served over steamed green beans. See the Ingredient Tip for how to check for (and remove) bones.

Serves: 2 to 3
Prep time: 10 minutes
Cook time: 20 minutes

1½ pounds fresh salmon (either a whole piece or three 8-ounce portions)
Salt
Freshly ground black pepper
¼ cup honey
2 tablespoons garlic paste
½ tablespoon ginger paste
1 tablespoon sesame oil
2 tablespoons soy sauce
1 tablespoon seasoned rice wine vinegar
1 teaspoon chili with garlic sauce, or sriracha

1. Preheat the oven to 375°F.
2. Season the salmon with just a little salt and black pepper and place it on a piece of aluminum foil twice as big as the fish. Curl the sides and ends of the foil up so that any sauce and juices will stay inside the foil.
3. In a small bowl, combine the honey, garlic paste, ginger paste, sesame oil, soy sauce, rice wine vinegar, and chili with garlic sauce and whisk until combined.
4. Spoon the sauce over the salmon, making sure to coat the entire surface with sauce.
5. Fold the sides of the foil up, leaving a 1-inch opening, and bake for 15 to 20 minutes.

Ingredient Tip: To find and remove pin bones, run your fingers down the middle of the salmon against the grain to feel for any missed bones. If you find any, use a pair of clean needle-nose pliers to remove and discard them.

Pro Tip: Reserve 1½ tablespoons of the sauce to drizzle on the salmon when there are just 5 minutes left of cooking time. To caramelize the top, open the foil and broil the salmon for 2 minutes.

Seared Scallops

SCALLOPS ARE SO SIMPLE TO MAKE. The trick is getting that perfect sear while not overcooking the scallops. Serve these over a bed of sautéed spinach or roasted asparagus. To change things up, serve over a quick Thai Curry Sauce (see the Swap It tip).

Serves: 2
Prep time: 5 minutes
Cook time: 5 minutes

10 to 12 scallops
Salt
Freshly ground black pepper
1 tablespoon olive oil

1. Heat a large nonstick frying pan or cast iron skillet over medium-high heat.
2. While the pan is heating, pat the scallops dry with a paper towel, then season them well with salt and black pepper.
3. Pour the olive oil into the pan. When the oil is shimmering, add the scallops one at a time, without crowding them, and cook for about 2 minutes per side, flipping them once.
4. Gently remove the scallops from the pan and plate.

Pro Tip: A perfect seared scallop should be nicely seared on the outside and buttery and translucent on the inside. If you are new to cooking scallops, purchase an extra scallop and do a test run. Bonus: You get to eat an extra scallop!

Swap It: Make a quick Thai Curry Sauce to go with the scallops. Combine ½ cup of your favorite store-bought tomato sauce with 6 tablespoons of coconut milk and 1 heaping tablespoon of Thai curry paste. Bring to a simmer over medium heat, then place a few spoonfuls on a plate and top with the scallops. Garnish with chopped chives and enjoy.

Linguini with Clams

I NEVER HAD LINGUINI AND CLAMS while growing up, or crabs for that matter. Let me tell you that once I discovered this dish, I was smitten. You *must* serve this with warm crusty bread to dip into the sauce. Delicious!

Serves: 3
Prep time: 10 minutes
Cook time: 15 minutes

---

2 tablespoons kosher salt

12 ounces linguini

6 tablespoons olive oil

3 garlic cloves, roughly chopped

1 (14-ounce) can diced tomatoes (preferably fire roasted)

¾ cup beer, or dry white wine

1 pound littleneck clams, cleaned (see Ingredient Tip)

1 teaspoon red pepper flakes

2 tablespoons chopped fresh parsley

1. Fill a large pot with water, add the salt, and bring to a rolling boil over high heat. Add the linguini and cook for 9 minutes. Remove the pot from the heat and carefully reserve ¼ cup of the pasta cooking water. Drain the linguini in a colander and set aside.
2. While the pasta is cooking, heat a large (12-inch or larger) sauté pan or pot over medium-high heat. Pour the olive oil into the pan and when it begins to shimmer, add the garlic and sauté for 30 seconds, stirring constantly.
3. Quickly add the tomatoes, beer, clams, and red pepper flakes. Give it a stir, then cover the pan and simmer for 5 minutes.
4. Remove the lid and continue to simmer another minute or two until the clams open.
5. Add the reserved pasta water and pasta to the pan and toss with tongs, coating the pasta with the sauce.
6. Sprinkle with the parsley and serve.

Ingredient Tip: If a clam has not opened after it has been cooked, discard it. Do not pry it open and try to eat it.

Take a Shortcut: In place of fresh clams, add 2 (6.5-ounce) cans of chopped clams and their liquid.

Clams 101: Clams, like mussels, are sold live because they spoil quickly after they're cooked. Ask your fishmonger to put the clams on ice for transport home. To clean clams, soak them in cold water for 30 to 40 minutes before using. The clams will breathe, expelling sand as they do. Lift the clams one by one to gently scrub off any debris found on the shells before cooking (this way, any expelled sand will remain in the bottom of the bowl and not end up in your food). Discard any chipped clams or any clams that do not close up when you disturb them.

Mussels in Red Sauce

WHO NEEDS TO GET DRESSED UP to go out to eat when you can make a dish like this at home? Making mussels is actually very easy. This dish can be served with linguini or fettuccini pasta or enjoyed as a light meal paired with a salad. It also makes a fun appetizer when served with garlic toast. Serving slices of toasted plain or garlic bread with these mussels is a must—you'll definitely want to sop up the flavorful sauce.

Serves: 2
Prep time: 10 minutes
Cook time: 10 minutes

2 tablespoons butter

½ cup chopped onion

4 large garlic cloves

½ cup white wine

1 (28-ounce) can diced tomatoes (preferably fire roasted)

Salt

Freshly ground black pepper

2 tablespoons chopped fresh parsley, plus more for garnish

Red pepper flakes or cayenne pepper (optional)

2 pounds mussels, scrubbed and debearded

Freshly shredded Parmesan cheese, for garnish (optional)

1. In a large skillet over medium-high heat, melt the butter. Add the onion and garlic and sauté for 4 minutes or until the onion is translucent but not browned.
2. Add the wine and tomatoes. Season with salt and black pepper.
3. Add the parsley and red pepper flakes (if using) and stir until combined.
4. Add the mussels, cover the pan with a lid, and simmer for 3 to 4 minutes.
5. Discard any mussels that have not opened, then serve, garnished with parsley and Parmesan cheese (if using).

Mussels 101: Mussels, like clams, are sold live because they spoil quickly after they're cooked. Ask your fishmonger to put the clams on ice for transport home. Look for shiny shells and mussels that are tightly shut. I like to buy an additional ½ pound or so of mussels to offset any that may not open; worst case scenario, you have extra to eat.

Put the mussels in a colander in the sink, run water over them and, using your hands, a clean brush, or a scrub sponge, rub off any debris, seaweed, sand, or barnacles. If a mussel does not close up as you do this, discard it because it is dead and inedible.

The "beard" of a mussel is the clump of hairlike fibers that sprouts from the shell. Farm-raised mussels often come debearded, but check and remove any beards that you find. To remove the beard, grab it and tug it off or use a knife to gently scrape it away.

Shrimp Nachos

THIS RECIPE DOESN'T REALLY NEED MEASUREMENTS. All you have to do is cook the shrimp, assemble the nachos, and add your chosen toppings. Make these nachos as simple or as loaded as you like. There is no right or wrong here. Enjoy them with ice cold beer or a pitcher of margaritas.

Serves: 4
Prep time: 10 minutes
Cook time: 10 minutes

1 cup guacamole (homemade [see Ingredient Tip] or store-bought)

½ pound raw shrimp, peeled, cleaned, and tails removed

2½ tablespoons blackening seasoning

1½ tablespoons olive oil

Tortilla chips

2 cups shredded Pepper Jack, Monterey Jack, Cheddar cheese, or a combination

1 jalapeño pepper, thinly sliced

¼ cup thinly sliced scallions

1 cup chopped grape tomatoes, or pico de gallo

⅓ cup sour cream

¼ cup chopped fresh cilantro

1. Preheat the oven to 400ºF degrees.
2. If making fresh guacamole, do so now.
3. Coat the shrimp in the blackening seasoning.
4. Heat a skillet over medium-high heat and pour in the olive oil. Once the oil begins to shimmer, add the shrimp and cook for 2 to 3 minutes per side or until pink and just cooked.
5. On a baking sheet or in a large cast iron pan or oven-safe pan, spread out the tortilla chips. Scatter the cheese, jalapeño pepper, scallions, and shrimp on top.
6. Place the baking sheet in the oven until the cheese is melted, then top with the guacamole, tomatoes, sour cream, and cilantro.

Ingredient Tip: Make a quick guacamole by roughly mashing together the flesh of 3 avocados, 1 teaspoon of lime juice, 1 minced garlic clove, and 1 minced jalapeño pepper. Season with salt.

Shopping Tip: Decide if you want to leave the shrimp whole. If so, purchase smaller shrimp (31 to 35 count); if you want to cut them into chunks, purchase 21 to 25 count. Precooked shrimp are not recommended for this dish because sautéing the shrimp adds so much flavor. For blackening seasoning, Chef Paul Prudhomme's Blackened Redfish Magic is just that: magic! You can usually find it in the spice aisle.

Parmesan Garlic Flounder

I LOVE FISH AND SEAFOOD. So much so that I am part of a seafood CSF, a program where you sign up to receive seafood on a weekly basis. It saves me time shopping and prompts me to try new things occasionally. When you're in a hurry, many varieties of fish and shellfish are a quick cooking option. This dish has a satisfying crunch and a nice flavor. You can use halibut, haddock, sea bass, or salmon in place of the flounder, although because those fish are typically thicker than flounder, they will take a little bit longer to bake.

Serves: 2
Prep time: 5 minutes
Cook time: 20 minutes

½ tablespoon olive oil

2 (6- to 8-ounce) pieces flounder

Salt

Freshly ground black pepper

2 garlic cloves, minced

¾ cup panko bread crumbs

½ cup grated Parmesan cheese

2 tablespoons butter, melted

1 lemon, cut into 4 wedges (optional)

1 tablespoon chopped fresh parsley, for garnish (optional)

1. Preheat the oven to 400°F. Brush a baking sheet with the olive oil (or spread it around with your fingertips).
2. Pat the flounder dry with a paper towel, season with salt and black pepper, and place the pieces on the baking sheet a few inches apart.
3. In a small bowl, combine the garlic, panko, and Parmesan, season with black pepper, and mix with a fork. Add the melted butter and mix until fully blended.
4. Using a spoon or your fingers, spread the breadcrumb mixture onto the fish, coating the entire top of each piece.
5. Bake for 15 to 20 minutes or until the fish is cooked through.
6. If you enjoy lemon on your fish, squeeze a wedge of lemon overtop, garnish with the parsley (if using), and enjoy.

Pro Tip: Never cook fish that is not fully thawed, and never attempt to defrost fish or shellfish in a microwave. Overall, when it comes to fish, fresh is best.

Swap It: To make this dish even faster, coat both sides of the flounder with the bread crumbs and pan fry them. Heat a large pan over medium-high heat, pour enough oil into the pan to coat the bottom, and once the oil is shimmering, add the fish and lower the heat to medium. Use a spatula to carefully turn the fish after 2 to 3 minutes and add a little more oil to the pan if necessary. Typically, flounder is thin, so it will cook through quickly.

8

Poultry

White Chicken Chili

I LOVE TRADITIONAL CHILI, but sometimes I want to change it up. That's when I opt for chicken chili. This chili can be made quickly using a store-bought rotisserie chicken. If you want to and have extra time, after you've pulled the meat off the chicken, wrap up the carcass, place in the refrigerator, and use it later to make your own chicken broth.

Serves: 4
Prep time: 10 minutes
Cook time: 20 minutes

1 tablespoon olive oil

¾ cup chopped onion

3 garlic cloves, minced

4 cups chicken broth

3 (14.5-ounce) cans
    cannellini beans, rinsed
    and drained

2 (4-ounce) cans
    chopped green chiles,
    or 1 to 2 fresh jalapeño
    peppers, minced

1 teaspoon ground cumin

½ tablespoon chili powder

½ teaspoon salt

Freshly ground black pepper

3 cups shredded
    rotisserie chicken

1. In a large pot, heat the olive oil over medium-high heat until it begins to shimmer.
2. Add the onion and sauté for 4 minutes until just tender. Add the garlic and sauté for another minute.
3. Add the chicken broth, beans, chiles, cumin, chili powder, and salt. Season with black pepper. Bring the chili to a boil.
4. Reduce the heat and allow the chili to simmer for 10 minutes.
5. Add the chicken to the pot, taste the chili, and adjust the seasoning to taste.

Swap It: Stir in ½ cup of heavy (whipping) cream at the end for more creaminess. Or purée 1 cup of the beans before adding them to the pot. If you enjoy spicy food and choose to use a fresh jalapeño or two, first taste the jalapeños for spice level and, if they are mild, include the seeds and maybe some cayenne pepper. If they are hot, start with 1 jalapeño and leave out the seeds.

Garlic Butter Chicken

THIS DISH IS SIMPLE BUT HAS GREAT FLAVOR. The browning of the chicken helps create a flavor base for both the sauce and the chicken. I like using sage for this dish although thyme is another delicious option. You can also use dried herbs, which will give the dish a slightly different flavor. Oven-Roasted Asparagus (page 58) and/or those 5-minute steamable potatoes (look in the produce section by the potatoes) are great accompaniments; you'll want to spoon some of the sauce over these as well.

Serves: 3 to 4
Prep time: 5 minutes
Cook time: 15 minutes

4 boneless, skinless chicken breasts

Salt

Freshly ground black pepper

1½ tablespoons olive oil

3 tablespoons butter

4 garlic cloves, minced

6 fresh sage leaves, chopped

½ cup white wine

Freshly squeezed lemon juice

1. If using chicken breasts that are thicker on one end than the other, use a mallet or rolling pin to pound the thicker side a few times to even them out to a ½-inch thickness throughout. If using breasts that are very large, slice them in half lengthwise.
2. Blot both sides of the chicken dry with paper towels, then season both sides well with salt and black pepper.
3. Heat a large (12-inch or larger) nonstick skillet over medium-high heat. Pour the olive oil into the skillet and once the oil begins to shimmer, add the chicken.
4. Cook the chicken for 5 to 6 minutes per side, flipping it with tongs, until it has a bit of a browned crust, then transfer to a plate.
5. Remove the skillet from the heat for 1 minute to let it cool down a bit.
6. Reduce the heat to medium, return the skillet to the heat, and put the butter in the skillet.
7. Add the garlic and sage and sauté for 30 seconds to 1 minute, being careful to not burn the garlic.
8. Add the wine and scrape up any bits from the bottom of the skillet.
9. Return the chicken to the skillet and spoon the sauce over the top. Serve with a spritz of lemon juice.

Shopping Tip: To reduce waste and save money, look for the small wrapped packages of poultry blend herbs, which have rosemary, thyme, and sage in the same package.

Sticky Chicken Meatballs

THIS SWEET AND SPICY SAUCE REMINDS ME a little of General Tso's, which is why I decided to pair it with chicken. The meatballs can be made the size of a typical meatball or as minis. You can enjoy them over rice, on a roll, or place a few on a baguette with pickled vegetables and make your own *bánh-mì*.

Serves: 4
Prep time: 10 minutes
Cook time: 15 minutes

1 pound ground chicken

¼ cup sliced scallions

4 garlic cloves, minced, or 4 tablespoons garlic paste, divided

¼ cup bread crumbs

Kosher salt

Freshly ground black pepper

½ cup ketchup

½ cup honey

3 tablespoons soy sauce

¼ cup brown sugar

1 tablespoon sesame oil

Olive oil

1. In a mixing bowl, combine the chicken, scallions, half the garlic, and bread crumbs. Season with salt and black pepper. Mix with your hands until the ingredients are well combined.
2. Form the mixture into balls about 2 inches in diameter and set aside.
3. In a saucepan over medium heat, combine the ketchup, honey, soy sauce, brown sugar, sesame oil, and remaining garlic. Bring to a simmer, whisking often. Remove from the heat and set aside.
4. In a nonstick frying pan over medium-high heat, heat enough olive oil to coat the bottom of the pan, and sauté the meatballs, moving them around until they are evenly browned. Add more olive oil if necessary.
5. Transfer the meatballs to the saucepan and simmer for a few minutes until the meatballs are cooked through.

Chicken and Dumplings

TALK ABOUT COMFORT FOOD. Chicken and dumplings is a Southern staple that has been around for hundreds of years. Traditionalists enjoy the doughy biscuits swimming in the rich and creamy broth, while others serve the dish with oven-baked biscuits atop the broth and chicken. Both ways are wonderful.

Serves: 4
Prep time: 10 minutes
Cook time: 20 minutes

4 bacon slices, chopped

4 boneless chicken thighs

Salt

Freshly ground black pepper

¼ cup all-purpose flour

¼ cup chopped onion

¼ cup chopped celery

5 cups chicken broth

1 cup frozen peas, or peas and carrots mix

1 cup heavy (whipping) cream

2 (10-ounce) tubes refrigerated biscuit dough, each biscuit cut into quarters

1. In a large pot or Dutch oven over medium-high heat, cook the bacon until crisp. Transfer the bacon to a paper towel–lined plate.
2. While the bacon cooks, season the chicken well with salt and black pepper, then dredge the chicken in the flour, shaking off any excess.
3. Add the chicken pieces to the pot over medium heat and cook for 3 to 4 minutes per side in the bacon fat until cooked through. Transfer the chicken to a cutting board.
4. Add the onion and celery to the pot, season with salt and black pepper, and sauté for 3 to 4 minutes.
5. Add the chicken broth and peas to the pot and scrape up any bits from the bottom of the pot with a spatula.
6. Slice or shred the chicken, then return it to the pot.
7. Reduce the heat to low, add the heavy cream, and allow it to simmer.
8. Drop the dough pieces into the broth, spacing them apart a bit, cover the pot, and cook for 6 to 8 minutes or until the dumplings are cooked through.
9. Season with salt and black pepper and serve.

Shopping Tip: Look for pre-chopped onions and celery to save time. You can often find them pre-cut in the same container.

Chicken Caprese

I WONDER IF THE PERSON who first came up with the combination of mozzarella, tomatoes, and basil knew just how popular it would be. Sure, these ingredients are amazing on their own as a salad, but combined with chicken, they make for a light, simple, and flavorful meal.

Serves: 4
Prep time: 10 minutes
Cook time: 15 minutes

2 tablespoons olive oil

1 teaspoon Italian seasoning, or dried oregano

1 teaspoon garlic powder

1 teaspoon salt

¼ teaspoon freshly ground black pepper

4 boneless, skinless chicken breasts

8 ounces fresh mozzarella (in ball form), cut into 8 slices

2 large ripe tomatoes, or 3 plum tomatoes, sliced about ½ inch thick

12 to 16 fresh basil leaves

¼ cup store-bought balsamic glaze

1. Preheat the oven to 375ºF.
2. In a small bowl, combine the olive oil, Italian seasoning, garlic powder, salt, and black pepper. Stir to combine and set aside.
3. If using chicken breasts that are thicker on one end than the other, use a mallet or rolling pin to pound the thicker side a few times to even them out to a ½-inch thickness throughout. If using breasts that are very large, slice them in half lengthwise. (You can use the extra chicken for another recipe or freeze it for later use if it has not been previously frozen.)
4. Coat the chicken all over with the olive oil mixture.
5. In a large oven-safe pan or cast iron skillet, cook the chicken breasts, turning once after about 5 minutes.
6. Top each chicken breast with 2 slices of mozzarella and pop the pan into the oven to melt the cheese, about 3 minutes.
7. Remove the pan from the oven and top with the tomato slices and basil leaves.
8. Drizzle with balsamic glaze and serve.

Ingredient Tip: Balsamic glaze is readily available in most grocery stores, typically in the same aisle as salad dressing or by the Italian specialty goods.

Barbecue Chicken Flatbread

SOMETHING ABOUT THE FLAVOR COMBINATION of chicken, barbecue sauce, red onions, and pizza dough makes me weak in the knees. You can make this flatbread with raw pizza dough, a ready-made pizza crust, or naan flatbread. This dish is also amazing when made with leftover pulled pork in place of the chicken.

Serves: 2
Prep time: 5 minutes
Cook time: 25 minutes

Nonstick cooking spray

2 boneless, skinless chicken breasts

1 teaspoon salt

½ teaspoon freshly ground black pepper

½ teaspoon garlic powder

1 tablespoon olive oil

1 cup barbecue sauce, plus more for drizzling

1 (8- to 10-inch) naan or 4 smaller flatbreads

¾ cup shredded Mexican cheese blend

¾ cup shredded mozzarella cheese

½ small red onion, thinly sliced

1. Preheat the oven to 400°F. Position the oven rack in the middle of the oven. Spray a baking sheet with cooking spray.
2. If using chicken breasts that are thicker on one end than the other, use a mallet or rolling pin to pound the thicker side a few times to even them out to a ½-inch thickness throughout. If using breasts that are very large, slice them in half lengthwise. (You can use the extra chicken for another recipe or freeze it for later use if it has not been previously frozen.)
3. Season the chicken with the salt, black pepper, and garlic powder.
4. Heat a nonstick skillet over medium-high heat and pour in the olive oil. Once the oil begins to shimmer, add the chicken and cook for about 3 minutes per side.
5. Transfer the chicken to a cutting board and brush both sides of the chicken with some barbecue sauce. Slice the chicken into strips.
6. Place the flatbread on the prepared baking sheet.
7. Spread some barbecue sauce on the flatbread, leaving a ½-inch clear edge.
8. Top the flatbread with the sliced chicken, Mexican cheese blend, mozzarella cheese, and onion slices.
9. Bake for 8 to 10 minutes or until the cheeses have melted.
10. Drizzle some additional barbecue sauce onto the flatbread. Slice and serve.

Chicken and Artichokes

SERVE THIS DISH WITH A LIGHT SALAD and either orzo or rice to enjoy with the sauce. The trick is to make sure you drain most of the liquid from the artichokes before adding them.

Serves: 3 to 4
Prep time: 5 minutes
Cook time: 25 minutes

4 boneless, skinless chicken breasts

Salt

Freshly ground black pepper

1 cup chicken broth

Juice of ½ lemon

1 tablespoon garlic paste or minced garlic

Red pepper flakes (optional)

1 tablespoon olive oil

⅓ cup minced onion

2 tablespoons butter

¼ cup heavy (whipping) cream

1 (14-ounce) can artichoke hearts, drained and patted dry

2 tablespoons fresh basil cut into ribbons, or thyme leaves

1. Preheat the oven to 375°F.
2. If using chicken breasts that are thicker on one end than the other, use a mallet or rolling pin to pound the thicker side a few times to even them out to a ½-inch thickness throughout. If using breasts that are very large, slice them in half lengthwise. (You can use the extra chicken for another recipe or freeze it for later use if it has not been previously frozen.)
3. Season both sides of the chicken generously with salt and black pepper and set aside.
4. In a small bowl, combine the chicken broth, lemon juice, garlic, and red pepper flakes (if using).
5. Heat the olive oil in a large oven-safe skillet over medium-high heat until it begins to shimmer. Add the chicken and brown it on both sides, 2 to 3 minutes per side (the chicken will finish cooking through in the oven).
6. Remove the chicken with tongs and transfer to a plate.
7. Reduce the heat to medium. Add the onion to the skillet and sauté for 2 minutes, then add the chicken broth mixture.
8. Scrape any brown bits from the bottom of the skillet and whisk. Raise the heat to medium-high and bring the mixture to a simmer for 5 to 6 minutes until the sauce has reduced by about half.
9. Once the sauce has thickened, turn off the stove and whisk in the butter until it melts into the sauce.
10. Whisk in the heavy cream, then return the chicken to the skillet, spooning some of the sauce over the top.
11. Nestle the artichokes into the sauce, spooning some over the tops of them, as well.
12. Bake for 10 minutes or until the chicken is cooked through.
13. Remove the skillet from the oven, sprinkle with the basil, and serve.

Chicken Quesadillas

QUESADILLAS ARE SIMPLE, hearty, and *so* fast to make that once you start making them at home, you're going to be doing it often. This is another recipe that, by using a store-bought rotisserie chicken or grilled chicken breasts, makes your life much easier. Top the quesadillas with salsa, guacamole, or sour cream for extra flavor.

Serves: 2
Prep time: 10 minutes
Cook time: 15 minutes

2 cups shredded
   rotisserie chicken

Salt

Freshly ground black pepper

1 tablespoon olive oil

1 green bell pepper, seeded
   and sliced

1 medium Vidalia
   onion, sliced

4 (6-inch) flour tortillas

1¼ cups of shredded
   Mexican cheese blend

Optional toppings: salsa,
   guacamole, sour cream

1. Season the chicken with salt and black pepper and set aside.
2. Heat a large nonstick pan or cast iron skillet over medium heat. Pour in the olive oil and when it begins to shimmer, add the bell pepper and onion and sauté for 4 to 5 minutes until tender. Remove the veggies and set aside.
3. Lay 1 tortilla on the pan, then spoon on half the pepper and onion mixture, half the chicken, then half the Mexican cheese blend.
4. Top with a second tortilla and allow it to continue cooking for about 2 minutes, putting pressure on it every now and again, until the tortilla is lightly browned.
5. Carefully and quickly flip the quesadilla over (you will need to use your free hand to help). Cook for an additional 1 to 2 minutes until the tortilla is lightly browned.
6. Remove from the heat and cut into quarters.
7. Repeat steps 4 through 8 to make the second quesadilla. Top with any or all of the optional toppings, and enjoy.

Ingredient Tip: If you want more of a "taco" flavor, season both the chicken and the vegetables with taco seasoning.

Honey Lime Chicken

IF YOU HAVE CHICKEN ON THE MENU a few nights a week, why not change it up with this simple, bright flavored sauce. Serve this dish with rice, green beans, or steamed broccoli. I like to save one of the breasts to slice and enjoy tossed with a salad for the next day's lunch or dinner.

Serves: 3 to 4
Prep time: 5 minutes
Cook time: 15 minutes

3 tablespoons honey

2 tablespoons soy sauce

3 tablespoons freshly
   squeezed lime juice

1 tablespoon garlic paste or
   1 garlic clove, minced

4 boneless, skinless chicken
   breasts or thighs

Salt

Freshly ground black pepper

2 tablespoons olive oil

2 tablespoons chopped
   fresh cilantro or parsley

1. Combine the honey, soy sauce, lime juice, and garlic paste in a small bowl or mason jar and whisk or shake until combined. Set aside.

2. If using chicken breasts that are thicker on one end than the other, use a mallet or rolling pin to pound the thicker side a few times to even them out to a ½-inch thickness throughout. If using breasts that are very large, slice them in half lengthwise. (You can use the extra chicken for another recipe or freeze it for later use if it has not been previously frozen.)

3. Pat the chicken dry with paper towels, then season well all over with salt and pepper.

4. Heat a skillet or sauté pan over medium-high heat and pour in the olive oil. When the oil begins to shimmer, add the chicken and cook until golden brown, 3 to 4 minutes per side.

5. Give the sauce another quick stir or shake, add it to the pan, and continue cooking another 6 to 10 minutes or until the chicken is cooked through.

Got Leftovers? Use any leftover chicken to top a salad or use for chicken salad.

Swap It: If you enjoy spicy food, add 1 tablespoon of chili with garlic sauce to the sauce mixture.

Sesame Noodles with Chicken

THIS IS ONE OF THE MOST POPULAR RECIPES in my family and circle of friends. It pretty much goes with everything and it's great for leftovers. I especially like to make it to accompany barbecued meats. The best part is that this is such an economical dish, so doubling it and taking it as your contribution to a gathering costs only a few dollars. Plus, people love the flavor; a double win!

Serves: 4
Prep time: 10 minutes
Cook time: 10 minutes

2 teaspoons salt

¾ cup soy sauce

2½ tablespoons red wine vinegar, or rice wine vinegar

3 tablespoons olive oil

¼ cup sesame oil

1½ tablespoons sugar

2 tablespoons chili with garlic sauce

1 pound linguini pasta

1 large red bell pepper

4 or 5 scallions, white and green parts

2 cups shredded rotisserie chicken

1. Fill a large pot with water, add the salt, and bring to a rolling boil over high heat.
2. While you wait for the water to boil, make the sauce by combining the soy sauce, red wine vinegar, olive oil, sesame oil, sugar, and chili with garlic sauce either in a jar with a lid or in a medium bowl. Shake or whisk vigorously to combine the ingredients.
3. Add the pasta to the boiling water and cook until al dente (still slightly chewy and firm to the bite), 6 to 7 minutes.
4. While the pasta is cooking, slice the bell pepper and scallions.
5. Drain the noodles in a colander, then blot them dry with paper towels.
6. Place the pasta and chicken in a large bowl, add the sauce, and use tongs to mix thoroughly. Serve.

Pro Tip: This dish is also delicious at room temperature or even cold. If you make this a few hours or even a day ahead, save half the sauce for just before you serve it, tossing to ensure all the pasta is "wet" with sauce.

Shopping Tip: Using a store-bought rotisserie chicken makes this dish come together fast. Use leftover chicken for chicken noodle soup (making a quick broth/stock from the chicken carcass and skin). Find sesame oil in the Asian section of the grocery store.

Turkey Burgers

MY POLISH GRANDMOTHER, WHO PASSED AWAY AT 102, was quite a creative home cook. It was she who introduced me to turkey burgers. She loaded them with mustard and added bread crumbs, so I do the same. These burgers are simple but wonderfully flavorful.

Makes: 4 burgers
Prep time: 10 minutes
Cook time: 10 minutes

---

1 pound ground turkey

2 tablespoons garlic paste or minced garlic

3 tablespoons chopped fresh parsley

½ cup fresh bread crumbs

1 tablespoon milk

1 egg yolk (see page 83 for how to separate eggs)

¼ teaspoon salt

⅛ teaspoon freshly ground black pepper

2 tablespoons grainy mustard (my favorite is Grey Poupon Country Dijon)

Rolls

Optional toppings: thinly sliced Pepper Jack, Monterey Jack, or fontina cheese; lettuce; sliced tomato

1. In a mixing bowl, combine the turkey, garlic paste, parsley, bread crumbs, milk, egg yolk, salt, black pepper, and mustard. Mix with your hands until just incorporated (do not overmix).
2. Form the mixture into 4 patties, pressing hard to form them as you would when making a snowball.
3. Place the burgers on a plate and, using your thumb or knuckle, make a divot right in the center of each burger, like a deep thumbprint but circular. This helps the burger cook more evenly and not puff up.
4. When ready to cook, either heat 1 tablespoon of oil in a skillet and pan fry the burgers over medium-high heat, or grill them.
5. The trick with turkey burgers is to not overcook them. Cook for 4 to 5 minutes per side, carefully flipping them once, and never pressing down on the burger.
6. If topping the burgers with cheese, do so when there is a minute or two of cooking time left to go.
7. Serve on rolls with more mustard and with any or all of the optional toppings.

Swap It: You can add some heat to these burgers by adding a minced jalapeño pepper to the burger mixture.

Turkey Lettuce Wraps

THIS IS A FAMILY FAVORITE that's great for busy weeknights. Leftovers reheat well and make for a tasty lunch. I also like to chop up the lettuce, spoon the turkey mixture over the top, add a sprinkling of peanuts, and enjoy it as a bowl. You can also serve this over rice.

Serves: 4
Prep time: 10 minutes
Cook time: 15 minutes

¼ cup soy sauce

¼ cup ketchup

1 tablespoon rice
    wine vinegar

4 teaspoons sesame oil

3 tablespoons brown sugar

1 teaspoon cornstarch

1 tablespoon olive oil

½ cup diced Vidalia onion

2 teaspoons minced garlic

1 pound ground turkey

1 head iceberg lettuce,
    core removed,
    leaves separated, or
    1 head romaine lettuce
    separated into leaves

1. In a small bowl, combine the soy sauce, ketchup, rice wine vinegar, sesame oil, and brown sugar and whisk until combined.
2. Take 2 tablespoons of sauce and place in a ramekin or small bowl. Mix in the cornstarch with a fork, forming a slurry, which will thicken the sauce. Set aside.
3. In a large pot, heat the olive oil over medium-high heat. When the oil begins to shimmer, add the onion and garlic and sauté for 3 minutes, stirring often.
4. Add the ground turkey, stirring often to break it up and allow it to brown evenly. Keep stirring until the turkey is no longer pink, 4 to 5 minutes.
5. Pour the sauce mixture into the pot. Stir and allow it to start bubbling.
6. Scrape in the cornstarch slurry and allow the mixture to bubble and thicken for a few minutes, then remove from the heat.
7. Spoon the filling into large lettuce leaves and wrap them burrito-style.

Swap It: If you enjoy spicy food, add ¼ teaspoon of red pepper flakes or ½ tablespoon of chili with garlic sauce. If you have peanuts, add in ½ cup for added texture. These can be added just as you remove the filling from the heat.

Stuffed Portabellas

PORTABELLAS ARE A FANTASTIC MUSHROOM for oven roasting or grilling. They're also great to stuff with meat, cheese, or rice. Serve these stuffed mushrooms on a bed of Sautéed Spinach (page 54) or over a spoonful of red pasta sauce for a light meal. A crisp glass of white wine would make a perfect pairing.

Serves: 2
Prep time: 10 minutes
Cook time: 20 minutes

4 large portabella mushrooms

2 tablespoons olive oil, plus more for cooking

Salt

Freshly ground black pepper

½ to ¾ pound ground turkey

½ cup chopped Vidalia onion

2 garlic cloves, minced

1 cup shredded mozzarella or gouda cheese

1. Preheat the oven to 375°F.
2. Clean the mushrooms by first brushing off any dirt with a dry paper towel. Next, break off the stems and set them aside. Use a spoon to carefully scrape out and discard the gills.
3. Brush all sides of the mushroom caps with the olive oil and season with salt and black pepper. Place them on a baking sheet or in a casserole dish.
4. Cut off and discard the thin, dry part of the mushroom stems. Chop up the rest of the stems and set aside.
5. Heat a skillet or sauté pan over medium-high heat. Pour in enough oil to coat the bottom of the skillet. When the oil begins to shimmer, add the ground turkey. Season with salt and black pepper and cook, stirring often, until the turkey is no longer pink.
6. Drain any liquid, transfer the turkey to a bowl tented with aluminum foil, and lightly wipe out the skillet with a paper towel.
7. Place the baking sheet with the mushroom caps into the oven for 8 to 10 minutes.
8. While the mushroom caps are cooking, return the skillet to the heat, pour in 1 tablespoon of oil, and add the onion. Sauté for 3 minutes. Add the garlic and sauté for 1 minute.

9. Add the chopped mushroom stems, season liberally with salt and black pepper, and sauté for just a few minutes until the mushrooms are soft. Drizzle a little more olive oil into the skillet if the mixture starts to look dry.

10. Remove the skillet from the heat, return the turkey to the skillet, and toss to combine.

11. Take the mushrooms out of the oven, spoon some of the mixture into each mushroom, and bake for an additional 8 to 13 minutes (depending on the size of the mushrooms and your preference for doneness).

12. A few minutes before the mushrooms are cooked, top each with ¼ cup of shredded mozzarella or gouda cheese and return to the oven to melt.

Thanksgiving Balls

YOU WILL NOT WANT TO WAIT for Thanksgiving leftovers to enjoy these babies. These are a very popular menu item at my local pub, and it was love at first bite for many people I know. These balls are extremely simple to make; all you need are mashed potatoes, stuffing, and turkey, plus some gravy to go on top. If you're like many of my friends, you will also want a side of cranberry sauce.

Serves: 4
Prep time: 10 minutes
Cook time: 15 minutes

2 cups leftover mashed potatoes

2 cups leftover moist stuffing

1½ cups leftover shredded or chopped turkey

Salt

Freshly ground black pepper

1 tablespoon chopped sage

½ tablespoon minced fresh thyme

Turkey gravy, warmed

Cranberry sauce

1. Preheat the oven to 350°F. Lightly oil a baking sheet.
2. In a mixing bowl, combine the mashed potatoes, stuffing, and turkey. Season well with salt and black pepper. Add the sage and thyme and mix until incorporated.
3. Form the mixture into balls (like a meatball) and place on the prepared baking sheet.
4. Bake for 10 to 12 minutes or until the exterior of the balls are just a little bit crispy.
5. Cover the balls with warmed turkey gravy and serve with a spoonful of cranberry sauce.

Ingredient Tip: If you are using leftover homemade gravy for this, you can omit the sage and thyme.

Take a Shortcut: If you do not have leftovers, you can use store-bought mashed potatoes and boxed stuffing. It will still be delicious. To mimic leftover turkey, purchase turkey cutlets or a turkey breast, season and oven roast it in an aluminum foil pouch, vented at the top, at 375°F until done.

9

Pork and Beef

Blackened Pork Tenderloin

THIS IS A GREAT DINNER paired with a Caesar salad and either green beans, asparagus, or rice. Searing the pork first before placing it in the oven seals in moisture and also creates a crisp exterior—and the result is fantastic.

Serves: 2
Prep time: 5 minutes
Cook time: 25 minutes

1 (1- to 1½-pound) pork
   tenderloin
Salt
Freshly ground black pepper
2 to 3 tablespoons
   blackening seasoning
2 tablespoons olive oil

1. Preheat the oven to 350°F. Allow the pork tenderloin to sit on the counter (unopened) for 30 minutes to come up to room temperature, which will allow for more even cooking.
2. When ready to cook, pat the tenderloin dry with paper towels, season it with salt and black pepper, and then pat the blackening seasoning evenly over the whole tenderloin.
3. Heat a large skillet or frying pan over medium-high heat, then pour in the olive oil. When the oil begins to shimmer, add the pork (you should hear it hit the pan with a nice sizzle).
4. Cook on each side for 2 minutes. Then, using tongs, sear the ends of the tenderloin for 45 to 60 seconds each. Add additional oil if needed.
5. If the pan is oven safe, place it in the oven. If not, transfer the pork to a baking dish and roast for 15 to 20 minutes (depending on the size of the tenderloin) or until the internal temperature reaches 145°F.
6. Allow the meat to rest for a few minutes before slicing.

Got Leftovers? I never heat up leftover meat because I feel it will become overcooked. I love it cold, sliced on its own or used in a sandwich.

Pork Bolognese

THIS IS COMFORT FOOD in a bowl for me and one of my favorite dinners in cooler months. Use a red wine you would enjoy drinking, not a cooking wine, for this. Serve warm crusty bread alongside for dipping into the sauce.

Serves: 4
Prep time: 5 minutes
Cook time: 25 minutes

1 tablespoon olive oil, or bacon grease

½ cup chopped Vidalia onion

¼ cup chopped carrots

Kosher salt

Freshly ground black pepper

2 large garlic cloves, minced

1 pound ground pork

4 ounces tomato paste

¾ cup red wine

2 tablespoons water

½ teaspoon dried or fresh thyme leaves

Rigatoni pasta, or your favorite pasta

Red pepper flakes (optional)

Freshly shaved Parmesan cheese (optional)

1. Heat the olive oil in a large pot over medium-high heat and add the onion and carrots. Sauté for 5 minutes or until the vegetables are tender and just browning.
2. Season well with salt and black pepper.
3. Add the garlic and sauté for 1 minute. Add the pork, breaking it up with a wooden spoon and allowing it to brown.
4. Add the tomato paste and stir it in. Add the wine, water, and thyme.
5. Season with additional salt and black pepper.
6. Turn the heat down to low and allow the sauce to simmer for 15 to 20 minutes, checking often to stir and add more liquid (water or wine) if needed.
7. While the sauce is cooking, fill a large pot with water, add salt, and bring to a rolling boil over high heat. Add the pasta and cook until al dente (still slightly chewy and firm to the bite), 6 to 7 minutes. Drain the pasta in a colander and set aside.
8. Add a few shakes of red pepper flakes (if using) to the sauce.
9. Serve the sauce over the pasta and sprinkled with Parmesan (if using).

Shopping Tip: Often in the produce section you can find small containers of mixed chopped vegetables, such as carrots, celery, and onions, which will save you prep time. Adding celery to this dish is perfectly fine.

Swap It: You can substitute beef or chicken for the pork; however, in my opinion the pork yields the best flavor.

Bacon Fried Rice

THIS BACON FRIED RICE tastes just as good, or better, than take out because, well . . . bacon! If you have an issue with gluten, there are a few varieties of gluten-free soy sauces, or you can swap out the soy sauce for tamari.

Serves: 4
Prep time: 10 minutes
Cook time: 10 minutes

8 bacon slices, chopped

½ cup chopped onion

1 cup peas, frozen or fresh

1 large garlic clove, minced

3 eggs, lightly beaten

3 cups cold cooked
   white rice

2 teaspoons sesame oil

3 tablespoons soy sauce

2 or 3 scallions, thinly sliced

1. In a large deep skillet or wok over medium-high heat, cook the bacon until crisp. Scoop out the bacon (leaving the bacon fat in the skillet) and place it on a paper-towel–lined plate.
2. Add the onion and peas to the skillet and sauté for 2 to 3 minutes.
3. Add the garlic and sauté for another minute.
4. With a spatula, move the vegetable mixture to one side of the skillet and pour the eggs into the free side, scrambling them until they are cooked, about 2 minutes, then stir everything together.
5. Add the rice, bacon, and sesame oil to the skillet and cook it through for a couple of minutes. Turn off the heat, add the soy sauce and scallions, and toss well.

Pro Tip: Cook the rice the day before you make this dish, or early enough that it has the chance to completely cool down and, if possible, be refrigerated. Using warm or hot rice will result in soggy rice, and that's no fun!

Shopping Tip: There are multiple varieties of rice that take just 2 minutes to cook in the microwave and taste great. They are perfect for this recipe if you don't happen to have leftover rice on hand.

Swap It: In place of bacon, you can use leftover ham, chicken, or pork.

Sausage and Peppers

GROWING UP IN PHILLY, there were a few foods always on rotation: cheesesteaks, roasted pork sandwiches, and sausage and peppers. For me, one of the best parts of a Phillies game was sitting in the stands with the intoxicating scent of sausage and peppers drifting through the air. This is one of my husband's favorite meals.

Serves: 4
Prep time: 5 minutes
Cook time: 25 minutes

1 tablespoon olive oil

2 pounds sweet or
  hot sausage

1 large sweet onion, sliced

3 bell peppers, sliced
  and seeded

2 garlic cloves, chopped

½ cup white wine

16 ounces tomato sauce

1. Heat a large 2-inch deep skillet or sauté pan over medium-high heat.
2. Pour in the olive oil, add the sausage, and cook until browned on all sides, about 10 minutes. Transfer the sausage to a plate.
3. Add the onion and bell peppers to the skillet and sauté for 5 minutes, adding a drizzle of additional oil if necessary.
4. While the vegetables are cooking, slice the sausage into 1-inch disks.
5. Add the garlic to the onion and peppers and sauté for 1 minute.
6. Pour the wine into the skillet and use a wooden spoon to scrape up any brown bits from the bottom of the skillet.
7. Add the tomato sauce and sausage slices and stir well. Cover the skillet with a lid, reduce the heat to low, and simmer for 10 minutes.

Ingredient Tip: You can use green, red, yellow, or orange bell peppers for this *or* use a variety of peppers.

Pro Tip: You can make a double batch and freeze half for up to 3 months. Simply defrost and reheat in the oven at 375°F for 15 to 20 minutes.

Gnocchi and Chorizo

I JUST LOVE A SATISFYING ONE-POT DINNER that comes together quickly, especially after a long day. Serve warm crusty bread alongside this meal to sop up the sauce, and maybe pair with a glass of wine. If you enjoy spicy food, add some red pepper flakes to give this dish some heat.

Serves: 2 to 3
Prep time: 10 minutes
Cook time: 15 minutes

1 tablespoon olive oil

½ cup diced onion

4 large garlic
cloves, chopped

½ pound loose chorizo

¼ cup chicken broth

1 (1-pound) package dry
potato gnocchi

1 roasted red pepper from a
jar, patted dry

1 (8-ounce) package
baby spinach

Freshly ground black pepper

½ cup shredded mozzarella
cheese (optional)

1. In a large nonstick skillet over medium-high heat, heat the olive oil. When it begins to shimmer, add the onion and sauté for 1 minute. Add the garlic and sauté for 5 seconds.
2. Add the chorizo and break it up with a spatula or wooden spoon, moving it around until browned.
3. Add the chicken broth and gnocchi, stir to incorporate, and cover the skillet with a lid for 2 to 3 minutes or until the gnocchi fluff up (most dry gnocchi only take 2 minutes to cook).
4. Remove the skillet from the heat, stir in the spinach, and season with black pepper to taste.
5. Top with the mozzarella cheese (if using).

Got Leftovers? If you have leftover raw chorizo or sausage, sauté it in a pan, drain any excess liquid, toss in mozzarella cheese, and mix until melted. Wrap it in pizza dough (that you cut into pieces and stretch to fit) to make what I call Sausage Bombs—they are unbelievable! Bake at 400°F for 15 to 20 minutes or until the dough is golden brown in spots, like a pizza crust.

Swap It: Use fresh cheese- or chicken-filled tortellini instead of gnocchi, or swap the chorizo for sweet or hot sausages with their casings removed. Swap the roasted red pepper for sun-dried tomatoes.

Lemon Pepper Pork Chops

THIS RECIPE WAS GIVEN TO ME by my friend Janet back when I was a beginner in the kitchen; it soon became one of my favorite fast dinners. I pair these chops with steamed green beans or broccoli and make drop biscuits to sop up the sauce. Depending on the size of the chops, this dish will serve 2 to 4. You may find yourself making extra sauce—it's just that tasty. If you want to do that, simply double the amounts of butter, mustard, and Worcestershire sauce.

Serves: 2 to 4
Prep time: 5 minutes
Cook time: 15 minutes

---

4 boneless pork chops

Lemon pepper seasoning

3 tablespoons
   butter, divided

1 tablespoon grainy
   Dijon mustard

1 tablespoon
   Worcestershire sauce

1. Dust both sides of the pork chops with lemon pepper seasoning.
2. Heat a nonstick sauté pan or skillet (with sides) over medium-high heat. Put 2 tablespoons of butter in the pan to melt.
3. Add the chops and cook until almost done (flipping them once). The cook time will depend on the size and thickness of the chops, but average chops will take 4 to 5 minutes per side. Check with a meat thermometer that the interior temperature has reached 145ºF.
4. Remove the pan from the heat, remove the chops, and place them on a plate tented with aluminum foil.
5. Add the remaining 1 tablespoon of butter, mustard, and Worcestershire sauce. Whisk until combined, then return the chops to the pan, and the pan to the heat for 1 minute more.

Ingredient Tip: You can easily find lemon pepper seasoning at the grocery store in the spice section.

Swap It: You can stir a tablespoon or two of heavy (whipping) cream into the sauce to increase the amount of sauce or make it creamier.

Quick Chili

CHILI IS ONE OF THE ULTIMATE COMFORT FOODS. It's not difficult to make and comes together quickly. Once you start making chili, you will begin to personalize it, and in no time you'll be making it without a recipe. There are probably as many chili variations as there are states. This is how we do it in my part of Pennsylvania. (Use two cans of beans if you love them or are trying to stretch the chili.)

Serves: 4
Prep time: 5 minutes
Cook time: 20 minutes

1 tablespoon olive oil

¾ cup chopped Vidalia onion

2 large garlic cloves, minced

1 pound ground beef

½ pound loose hot Italian sausage (or links, casings removed and sausage broken up)

½ cup dark beer

1 (28-ounce) can crushed tomatoes

3 tablespoons tomato paste

4 tablespoons chili powder

1½ teaspoons salt

1 teaspoon freshly ground black pepper

1 tablespoon Worcestershire sauce

1 or 2 (16-ounce) cans kidney beans, rinsed and drained

Optional toppings: shredded Cheddar cheese, sour cream, chopped scallions

1. Heat the olive oil in a large pot over medium heat until it begins to shimmer. Add the onion and garlic and sauté, stirring often, for about 2 minutes.
2. Scrape the mixture into a small bowl and set aside.
3. Add the ground beef and sausage to the pot and cook over medium-high heat, adding a little oil if necessary. Cook, stirring often, until the meat is mostly browned. Drain most of the grease/liquid into a bowl or mug to be discarded in the trash once cooled (never down the drain).
4. Add the beer. Scrape the onion mixture back into the pot and simmer for 2 minutes.
5. Add the tomatoes and tomato paste. Stir well. Add the chili powder, salt, black pepper, Worcestershire sauce, and kidney beans. Stir well.
6. Let the chili come to a bubble, stirring often. Reduce the heat to low and continue cooking for 10 to 15 minutes, stirring often.
7. Taste and adjust the seasoning to your liking. Serve as is or with any of the optional toppings.

Got Leftovers? Top a baked potato with chili and call it dinner. Use leftover chili to make nachos or just enjoy it using tortilla chips as your spoon. Warm chili and top it with a fried egg or two for breakfast.

Swap It: If you like chunks of tomato in your chili, swap crushed tomatoes for diced. Enjoy hot and spicy chili? Add a chopped jalapeño pepper or two or swap out traditional chili powder with ancho chili powder.

Philly Cheesesteak

AS A GIRL BORN AND RAISED IN PHILLY, I could write a small book on cheesesteak. "Wit or witout" . . . Pat's or Geno's . . . You do you and put on what you enjoy. I have had cheesesteaks made with frozen Steak-Um meat and with filet mignon and with everything in between, and they're all good. My perfect cheesesteak is actually more of a cheesesteak hoagie; I want my meat and cheese nestled atop shredded lettuce, on a mayo-smeared soft hoagie roll, and topped with a handful of hot pepper rings. Now, my mom? She wants the meat and cheese slathered in pizza sauce on an oven-crisped roll with fried onions. See? You do you!

Serves: 2
Prep time: 5 minutes
Cook time: 10 minutes

1¼ pounds boneless short ribs or rib-eye

2 soft hoagie rolls

Olive oil

Salt

Freshly ground black pepper

6 pieces American cheese (or provolone or Cheez Whiz)

Optional toppings: pepperoni slices, sautéed mushrooms, sautéed onions and/or peppers, shredded lettuce, sliced tomatoes, pizza sauce, sweet or hot peppers, mushrooms

1. Pop the meat in the freezer for 30 to 45 minutes before you plan on cooking. If the meat is partially frozen, slicing it thinly is much easier. Thinly sliced meat is the foundation of the Philly cheesesteak.
2. Cut the partially frozen meat into thin strips. The size of the strips doesn't really matter; it's all about the thinness.
3. Slice the rolls (if you want them toasted, now's the time to pop them in a hot oven for a few minutes or, as they do in Philly pizza shops, lay them face-down on a hot griddle).
4. Heat a large frying pan, sauté pan, or griddle over medium-high heat and pour in enough olive oil to coat the bottom of the pan.
5. Once the oil begins to shimmer, add the thinly sliced meat and season with a generous pinch of salt and black pepper. Cook the meat, moving it around quickly, until it's cooked through, about 5 minutes.
6. Divide the meat into two portions in the pan and place 3 slices of cheese on top of each section of meat, covering all the meat if possible. Cover the pan with a lid, remove the pan from the heat, and in a minute or less the cheese should be melted.
7. Use a spatula to swipe up one portion of meat and cheese and fill the roll with it. Top with any of the optional toppings you like, or choose your own.

Roasted Red Pepper Mushroom and Steak Flatbread

FLATBREADS HAVE BEEN ALL OVER MENUS from pubs to fine dining the past couple of years, and I can see why. They are easy to assemble and so versatile. This easy flatbread pairs wonderfully with red wine and is perfect for a date night. Double the recipe and it also works as an appetizer when entertaining.

Serves: 2
Prep time: 15 minutes
Cook time: 5 minutes

6 ounces dried mushrooms (chanterelles, porcini, or shiitake)

1 (¾- to 1-pound) steak (strip, rib-eye, or filet)

Kosher salt

Freshly ground black pepper

1 tablespoon olive oil

1 (8- to 10-inch) naan or 4 smaller flatbreads

2 cups shredded provolone cheese, divided

1 (12-ounce) jar roasted red peppers, drained, dried, and cut into strips

¼ cup snipped scallions

Fresh thyme leaves, for garnish (optional)

Balsamic glaze, for garnish (optional)

1. Preheat the oven to 350°F.
2. Rehydrate the mushrooms according to the package directions (this will generally involve soaking them in water for up to 30 minutes).
3. Season the steak liberally with salt and black pepper.
4. Heat a heavy skillet or cast iron pan over medium-high heat. Once the pan is hot, pour in the olive oil. When the oil begins to shimmer, sear the steak and cook to rare (2 to 3 minutes per side or until the internal temperature reaches 125°F; don't cook much beyond rare, because the sliced steak will be going into the oven for a few minutes). Let the steak rest for 5 minutes and then slice it into strips.
5. Place the naan on a baking sheet and assemble the flatbread by scattering 1½ cups of provolone cheese over the naan, followed by the mushrooms, roasted red peppers, scallions, and steak slices. Scatter the remaining ½ cup of cheese on top.
6. Place in the oven just until the cheese melts, 2 to 3 minutes.
7. Garnish with thyme and a drizzle of balsamic glaze (if using).

Ingredient Tip: Feel free to use other varieties of flatbread for this recipe. Just don't use something as thin as tortilla wraps.

Ground Beef Stir Fry

THERE IS SOMETHING ABOUT THESE FLAVORS that makes me want to enjoy them over and over again. This stir fry is a family favorite and a definite go-to on busy weeknights. The key to success is to have all the ingredients prepped before you begin cooking. Serve this stir fry over rice or enjoy it as is for a low-carb meal.

Serves: 3 to 4
Prep time: 10 minutes
Cook time: 15 minutes

2 tablespoons olive oil, divided

½ pound fresh green beans, cut into 1-inch pieces

½ cup finely chopped onion

2 tablespoons minced garlic

1 tablespoon minced fresh ginger

1 pound ground beef

¼ cup soy sauce

2 tablespoons mirin

1 tablespoon chili with garlic sauce

1 tablespoon sesame oil

Snipped scallions, for garnish

Chopped peanuts, for garnish (optional)

Cooked jasmine, basmati, or white rice, for serving (optional)

1. Heat a skillet over medium-high heat. Once the skillet is hot, pour in 1 tablespoon of olive oil and the green beans.
2. Allow the green beans to begin to char, stirring them occasionally (they will sizzle and pop and that is okay). You want the beans to remain crisp-tender, about 3 minutes. Remove the green beans from the skillet and set aside.
3. Add the remaining 1 tablespoon of oil and the onion to the skillet and sauté for 2 minutes, then add the garlic and ginger and stir for 30 seconds.
4. Add the ground beef, using a spatula to break it up and mix it in with the onions, and cook it through, about 10 minutes.
5. If any excess liquid accumulates, drain it into a bowl or mug to be discarded in the trash once cooled (never down the drain).
6. While the meat cooks, combine the soy sauce, mirin, chili with garlic sauce and sesame oil in a bowl or mason jar and whisk until incorporated.
7. Add the sauce to the beef and heat through until bubbly.
8. Remove the skillet from the heat and garnish with scallions and/or chopped peanuts (if using). Serve as is or over rice.

Swap It: You can swap the ground beef for ground chicken, turkey, veal, or pork.

Skillet Steak and Potatoes

MY FATHER WAS ALL ABOUT MEAT and potatoes for dinner when he came home from work. This is one meal we had often growing up; however, back then they made it in an electric frying pan that sat right on the dinner table. If that pan could talk! This is a robust meal that is full of flavor and made for a glass of red wine.

Serves: 2
Prep time: 15 minutes
Cook time: 15 minutes

---

2 tablespoons olive
  oil, divided

3 tablespoons soy sauce

2 tablespoons minced garlic

¾ pound flank steak

½ teaspoon onion powder

½ teaspoon garlic powder

¼ teaspoon salt

¼ teaspoon freshly ground
  black pepper

¾ pound fingerling potatoes,
  or other baby potatoes,
  cut into bite-size pieces

1 small onion, sliced

2 tablespoons
  butter, divided

½ tablespoon chopped
  fresh thyme

1. In a medium bowl, combine 1 tablespoon of olive oil, soy sauce, and garlic. Whisk to blend and set aside.
2. Slice the steak against the grain into ¾-inch-thick strips and place those slices in the marinade.
3. In a ramekin or small bowl, combine the onion powder, garlic powder, salt, and black pepper.
4. Season the potatoes well with the seasoning mixture.
5. Heat a large skillet over medium-high heat. Once the skillet is hot, pour in the remaining 1 tablespoon of oil, seasoned potatoes, and onion.
6. Cook the potatoes for 6 to 7 minutes, turning them occasionally, or until you can easily pierce them with a fork. Halfway through the cooking time, add 1 tablespoon of butter.
7. Remove the potatoes from the skillet and set aside.
8. Add the remaining 1 tablespoon of butter and the thyme and cook for 30 seconds.
9. Add the steak strips (reserve the marinade) and cook for 2 minutes, turning the meat once.
10. Add the marinade and potatoes and cook for another 2 minutes.
11. Following these timings, the steak strips should come out medium. If you prefer your steak more or less rare, adjust the cook time accordingly.

Swap It: If you do not enjoy onions, leave them out or swap them out for button mushrooms. If you love the flavor of rosemary, swap that out for the thyme. Just be sure to add one fresh herb, as its flavor makes the dish shine.

Beef and Broccoli

WHY ORDER OUT when you can whip this up at home? Plus, making favorite takeout dishes yourself is healthy, and you get to enjoy it fresh from the pan. This recipe is another one where you really need to have your mise en place in order. The cooking moves quickly, so the more organized you are before you cook, the better the result. Serve with sticky rice.

Serves: 4
Prep time: 10 minutes
Cook time: 10 minutes

3 tablespoons soy sauce

1½ tablespoons packed light brown sugar, or mirin

3 tablespoons sesame oil, divided

3 cups broccoli florets, cut into bite-size pieces

2 tablespoons minced garlic, divided

1 teaspoon grated or minced fresh ginger

1 pound flank or strip steak, cut into thin 1-inch pieces

Salt

Freshly ground black pepper

2 tablespoons cornstarch

1. In a small bowl, stir together the soy sauce and brown sugar.
2. In a large skillet or frying pan with high sides, heat 1 tablespoon of sesame oil.
3. Add the broccoli and cook for 3 to 4 minutes.
4. Add the garlic and ginger and cook for 1 minute more.
5. Transfer the contents of the skillet to a bowl. Wipe the skillet out a bit with a paper towel.
6. Season the steak strips with salt and pepper then dredge the strips in the cornstarch.
7. Add the remaining 2 tablespoons of oil to the skillet, turn the heat to medium-high, and once the oil begins to shimmer, add the steak strips and cook, stirring, for about 3 minutes. Don't crowd the steak; you may need to cook it in two batches.
8. Once the steak is cooked, return the broccoli mixture to the skillet and add the sauce. Bring it to a simmer, allowing the sauce to bubble and thicken, then serve.

New Orleans–Style Dirty Rice

THIS IS MY GO-TO RECIPE when I either can't or don't want to think up anything new to make for dinner, or when I need a quick protein-rich meal. Sure, you could start with plain white rice, add seasonings, and make the dirty rice yourself, but why do that when the name synonymous with Louisiana cooking already does it better? Zatarain's boxed dirty rice provides a great base for this dish and is enhanced by freshly sautéed ground pork.

Serves: 2 to 3
Prep time: 5 minutes
Cook time: 25 minutes

1 tablespoon olive oil

1 garlic clove, minced

1 pound ground pork

Salt

Freshly ground black pepper

Spicy Cajun seasoning (optional)

1 (8-ounce) box Zatarain's Dirty Rice

2 scallions, thinly sliced, for garnish (optional)

1. Heat a large sauté pan or skillet over medium-high heat. Pour in the olive oil and then the garlic and sauté for 1 minute, then add the ground pork.
2. Season with salt and black pepper (if you like spicy food, add ½ teaspoon or more of Cajun seasoning) and cook for 5 to 6 minutes until cooked through, using a wooden spoon or spatula to break up the pork as it cooks.
3. Drain off any excess liquid and set the pork aside.
4. While the pork is cooking, cook the rice according to the package instructions. When there are about 3 minutes left of the cooking time (and some liquid still remains in the pot), stir in the pork and cook until the liquid is absorbed.
5. Taste and add Cajun seasoning to taste.
6. Scrape into a serving bowl and top with the scallions (if using).

Swap It: Swap the pork for ground beef, ground turkey, sliced cooked turkey, or sliced pork sausage or andouille.

Steak with Chimichurri Sauce

IF I WAS A WAGERING GIRL, I'd bet you a dollar that if you have yet to taste chimichurri sauce, your first bite will have you doing the happy food dance. It's that much of a flavor explosion. This Argentine sauce is so easy to make, and not only does it go beautifully with steak, its vibrant flavors brighten up potatoes, chicken, shrimp, simple grilled fish, and more.

Serves: 4
Prep time: 10 minutes
Cook time: 15 minutes

1½ to 2 pounds steak
of your choice (see
Ingredient Tip)

1 bunch fresh
parsley, chopped

1 tablespoon chopped
fresh oregano, or
1 teaspoon dried

1 red chile pepper, chopped,
or ¼ to ½ teaspoon red
pepper flakes

4 garlic cloves, minced

½ cup olive oil, plus
1½ tablespoons

¼ cup red wine vinegar

¾ teaspoon salt, plus more
for seasoning the steak

Scant ½ teaspoon freshly
ground black pepper,
plus more for seasoning
the steak

1. Before you begin cooking, set the steaks out on the counter for 30 minutes to come to room temperature.
2. For the sauce: In a bowl, combine the parsley, oregano, red chile, and garlic.
3. Add the olive oil, red wine vinegar, salt, and black pepper and stir to combine. Let sit while you cook the steak.
4. Pat the steak dry with a paper towel and season the meat well on both sides with salt and black pepper.
5. Heat a cast iron pan or skillet over medium-high heat and pour in 1½ tablespoons of oil. Once the oil begins to shimmer, add the steak and cook for 3 to 5 minutes on each side for medium rare or 5 to 7 minutes on each side for medium. Add a little more oil if necessary.
6. Remove from the heat and allow the steaks to rest for a few minutes (they will continue to cook as they sit).
7. Spoon the chimichurri sauce over the steak and enjoy. You can serve the steak whole or slice it prior to spooning the sauce over for an elegant presentation.

Ingredient Tip: Choose your favorite cut of steak for this recipe. I almost always choose filet mignon or flank steak. My husband would choose a rib-eye or strip steak. For a special occasion, grill a whole tenderloin that's been coated in seasoned garlic oil (marinate 3 garlic cloves, ½ tablespoon of salt, and ½ teaspoon of freshly ground black pepper in ⅓ cup of olive oil for 1 hour, then coat the tenderloin with that). Oven roast or grill to perfection—in my world that's medium rare—and then spoon chimichurri sauce over the meat. Yum!

Pro Tip: Chimichurri can be made a day ahead of time.

10

Dessert in 15 Minutes or Less

Grilled Peaches

SOMETHING MAGICAL HAPPENS WHEN YOU GRILL PEACHES over an open flame or expose them to heat. Their natural sweetness shines and makes this one of the best desserts imaginable—yet it's so simple. Serve alone, with a scoop of vanilla ice cream, or with a dollop of fresh whipped cream or mascarpone cheese.

Serves: 2
Prep time: 5 minutes
Cook time: 5 minutes

2 peaches, halved and pits removed

½ tablespoon sugar

½ tablespoon melted butter

Optional toppings: honey, ice cream, whipped cream

1. Clean and oil the grill grates. Preheat the grill to medium high.
2. Sprinkle the peach halves with the sugar and allow them to sit while the grill heats.
3. Brush the cut sides of the peaches with the melted butter and grill face-down for 1 to 2 minutes, just until the peaches char a bit. Using tongs, flip them over and grill for another 1 to 2 minutes.
4. Remove the peaches from the grill and enjoy as is or with any of the optional toppings.

Pro Tip: You can also cook these indoors using a grill pan or broiling them for a couple of minutes.

Swap It: You can easily make these peaches your own by adding either a sprinkle of ground cinnamon or cardamom before cooking, using brown sugar in place of regular sugar, or drizzling with caramel sauce to serve.

Cannoli Dip

THIS RECIPE IS ALWAYS A HIT. If only people knew just how simple it is to make. You can serve this with broken-up cannoli shells, broken-up ice cream sugar cones, graham crackers, or strawberries.

Serves: 6
Prep time: 10 minutes

1 cup ricotta cheese, strained

4 ounces cream cheese

½ cup powdered sugar, plus more for dusting

1 teaspoon vanilla extract

¼ cup mini chocolate chips, plus more for garnish

1. Place the ricotta on a few paper towels and allow it to sit for a few minutes to drain, then pat it dry with additional paper towels as best you can. The drier the ricotta, the better. If you have a cheesecloth, use that in place of paper towels and squeeze the ricotta dry over the sink.
2. In the bowl of a stand mixer (or use a hand mixer), combine the ricotta, cream cheese, powdered sugar, and vanilla extract and whip for 2½ to 3 minutes.
3. Use a spatula to fold in the chocolate chips, then scrape the dip into a serving bowl. Garnish with a few more chips and dust with powdered sugar just before serving.
4. If making ahead of time, cover and refrigerate until ready to serve.

Shopping Tip: You can find cannoli shells in many grocery stores or at some pizza places and Italian markets.

Swap It: Use mascarpone cheese in place of the cream cheese and adjust the sugar to ⅓ cup. Use this to fill cannoli shells to make cannoli. Place mini chocolate chips on the ends where the filling sticks out, and dust with powdered sugar. Fill just before enjoying.

Sautéed Apples

ENJOY THESE APPLES ON THEIR OWN, over ice cream, or stirred into overnight oats or oatmeal. I also love them as a topping for pancakes or cheesecake. Not only are these apples easy to make, they also make the kitchen smell amazing!

Serves: 2
Prep time: 5 minutes
Cook time: 10 minutes

1 tablespoon butter, or coconut oil

1½ cups chopped Honeycrisp apples

½ tablespoon brown sugar

1 teaspoon vanilla extract

Scant ½ teaspoon ground cinnamon (more or less to taste)

2 pinches ground nutmeg

Freshly squeezed lemon juice

1. Heat a sauté pan over medium heat and melt the butter or coconut oil.
2. Toss in the apples, cover the pan, and cook the apples for a few minutes, stirring once or twice, adding ½ tablespoon of water if the pan becomes dry.
3. Add the sugar, vanilla extract, cinnamon, nutmeg, and a spritz of lemon juice, stir well, and sauté until the apples begin to soften and caramelize.
4. Taste and adjust the seasoning, adding a little more sugar or spice to taste.

Pro Tips: Cutting the apple chunks as close in size as possible allows them to cook evenly. You can leave the apple skin on or take it off.

Swap It: Swap the sugar for maple syrup, agave, or honey.

Warm Caramelized Bananas

TAKE THE HUMBLE BANANA UP A NOTCH with this recipe, which is a much simpler variation of Bananas Foster. The ooey-gooey sauce mingling with the bananas is pure comfort food. Depending on the banana's sugar content, you will end up with slightly caramelized bananas or warm bananas in a nice sauce. Either way, it's so tasty!

Serves: 2
Prep time: 5 minutes
Cook time: 6 minutes

3 tablespoons sugar

¼ teaspoon ground cinnamon

1½ tablespoons butter

2 large fresh bananas (not overripe), cut into ½-inch thick rounds

1. Combine the sugar and cinnamon in a medium bowl.
2. In a large nonstick pan over medium-high heat, melt the butter.
3. While the butter melts, quickly and gently toss the bananas in the cinnamon sugar mixture to coat them and then place them in the pan.
4. Allow the bananas to sit undisturbed for 2½ to 3 minutes. Use a small spatula to peek to see if they've browned a bit on the bottom. Carefully flip the bananas and cook for a further 2½ to 3 minutes.
5. If the bananas begin to burn, remove the pan from the heat, lower the heat, and flip the bananas before returning the pan to the heat. It's a fine balance when it comes to the cook time; too long and the bananas can end up mushy. Best to use a hot pan and quickly get them in, flipped, and out.
6. Scoop some warm banana slices onto ice cream or enjoy as is. These are best enjoyed right from the pan while still warm.

Swap It: Add pepitas, walnuts, or pecans for some delicious crunch.

Nutella Brownie Bites

NUTELLA HAS A CULT-LIKE FOLLOWING, and it's easy to understand why. It's perfect for when a chocolate craving strikes. These Nutella brownie bites remind me of little lava cakes. Make them bite-size or larger like a cupcake. Enjoy alone, with a dusting of powdered sugar, or with ice cream.

Serves: 4
Prep time: 5 minutes
Cook time: 10 minutes

1 cup Nutella

Nonstick cooking spray, or mini cupcake liners

¼ cup mini chocolate chips or chopped chocolate bar

½ cup all-purpose flour

2 eggs

1. Preheat the oven to 350°F. Spray a mini cupcake tin with cooking spray.
2. Place the Nutella in a microwave-safe medium bowl and warm it for 30 seconds, just enough to make it easier to stir (not hot).
3. Add the chocolate chips, flour, and eggs to the Nutella and mix well.
4. Spoon the mixture into the cups, filling each two-thirds full, and bake for 8 to 10 minutes. You want the centers just a little gooey. If you want them more solid, cook for an additional few minutes.
5. Pop them out and enjoy.

Note: You can also use a regular-size cupcake pan; just increase the cook time by a further 8 to 10 minutes.

Whipped Ricotta

ONE OF MY MOST FAVORITE FOODS EVER! I enjoy whipped ricotta both as a dessert and as an appetizer offering. It's perfect on a cheese board alongside fruit and slices of French bread. I also love it with chopped cooked fruit on top, such as the Grilled Peaches (see page 144). If you can find fresh whole milk ricotta from a local farm or farmers' market, it will change your world.

Serves: 4
Prep time: 10 minutes

16 ounces whole milk ricotta

3 tablespoons honey, plus more for drizzling

3 tablespoons chopped pistachios, or your favorite nuts (optional)

Pita chips or French bread, for serving

1. Place the ricotta in a mixing bowl. Add the honey and whip for 1 to 2 minutes until fluffy and smooth.
2. Scrape the ricotta onto a small platter, spread it out, and sprinkle the nuts on top or pile to one side (if using).
3. Drizzle with additional honey and serve with plain pita chips or thin slices of French or ciabatta bread.

Swap It: I love adding Sweet and Spicy Nuts to this. You can purchase them already made or use the recipe on page 49. You can also scatter a little fresh thyme overtop for a pop of color and flavor. Or you can make ricotta toast, similar to avocado toast.

Caramel Apple Dip

TAKE A CARAMEL APPLE TO A WHOLE NEW LEVEL with this incredibly delicious dip and watch people crowd around it. Serve with Honeycrisp, Red Delicious, Granny Smith, or a mix of your favorite apples.

Serves: 4
Prep time: 10 minutes

8 ounces cream cheese

3 tablespoons honey, or powdered sugar

1½ cups caramel dip

1 cup toffee pieces

3 apples, sliced

1. In a mixing bowl, beat together the cream cheese and honey until fully combined. Scrape the mixture into a small serving dish.
2. Top with the caramel, smoothing it evenly over the top of the cream cheese mixture.
3. Sprinkle the toffee chips on top and serve with the sliced apples.

Shopping Tip: Look for caramel apple dip in tubs in the produce section, typically near the apples.

Swap It: You can use chopped-up Heath Bar, chopped nuts, or chopped white or chocolate chips in place of plain toffee.

Chocolate Chip Mug Cookie

WHEN THE SWEET CRAVING HITS, you can enjoy this cookie in a mug in under 3 minutes. Really! It's warm and does the trick. Love nuts? Add a tablespoon of walnuts or top with a scoop of vanilla ice cream or whipped cream.

Serves: 1
Prep time: 5 minutes
Cook time: 1 minute

1 tablespoon butter

½ tablespoon sugar

½ tablespoon brown sugar

Pinch salt

1 teaspoon vanilla extract

1 egg yolk

2 tablespoons all-
   purpose flour

1 to 2 tablespoons
   chocolate chips

1. Put the butter in the mug you will use and melt it in the microwave for 35 to 45 seconds.
2. Add the sugar and brown sugar, salt, and vanilla extract to the melted butter and mix well.
3. Add the egg yolk and mix vigorously until it's completely incorporated.
4. Add the flour and mix until incorporated.
5. Stir in the chocolate chips.
6. Microwave undisturbed for 50 to 60 seconds, depending on the microwave.
7. Dig in!

Cookies and Cream Milkshake

WHEN IT COMES TO A MILKSHAKE, I say go big or go home—and what's more decadent than a cookies and cream milkshake topped with fresh whipped cream? Always try to use fresh whipped cream; it literally takes a minute to make and is *way* better than anything from the grocery store.

Serves: 2
Prep time: 10 minutes

8 Oreos or chocolate chip
 cookies
2½ cups vanilla ice cream
¼ cup whole milk
Whipped cream

1. Put the cookies in a blender and pulse until they are crumbs.
2. Add the ice cream and milk and blend until smooth.
3. Scrape the mixture into glasses and top with whipped cream.

Whipped Cream and Berry Trifles

NEED A PRETTY DESSERT IN A HURRY? This one fits the bill. The trifle has been around since the early 18th century, and one taste of its fresh, bright flavors will tell you why. Use store-bought sponge cake, pound cake, angel food cake, or madeleines along with fresh berries and homemade whipped cream. Serve in wine glasses or mason jars for individual desserts, or make as a larger dessert in a trifle or glass bowl.

Serves: 4
Prep time: 5 minutes

8 ounces heavy
   (whipping) cream
½ teaspoon vanilla extract
3 tablespoons
   powdered sugar
Store-bought pound cake or
   angel food cake
2 cups chopped
   strawberries, plus
   4 whole berries for
   garnish

1. Whip the heavy cream in a stand mixer or with a hand mixer on high for 30 to 45 seconds. Add the vanilla extract and powdered sugar and beat for another 15 seconds (a few seconds longer if using a hand mixer) or until the whipped cream has stiff peaks. Set aside.
2. Cut the cake into bite-size pieces.
3. In 4 wineglasses or mason jars, layer the cake pieces, chopped berries, and whipped cream. Garnish with a whole strawberry.

Measurement Conversions

VOLUME EQUIVALENTS (LIQUID)

US STANDARD	US STANDARD (OUNCES)	METRIC (APPROXIMATE)
2 TABLESPOONS	1 FL. OZ.	30 ML
¼ CUP	2 FL. OZ.	60 ML
½ CUP	4 FL. OZ.	120 ML
1 CUP	8 FL. OZ.	240 ML
1½ CUPS	12 FL. OZ.	355 ML
2 CUPS OR 1 PINT	16 FL. OZ.	475 ML
4 CUPS OR 1 QUART	32 FL. OZ.	1 L
1 GALLON	128 FL. OZ.	4 L

OVEN TEMPERATURES

FAHRENHEIT (F)	CELSIUS (C) (APPROXIMATE)
250°	120°
300°	150°
325°	165°
350°	180°
375°	190°
400°	200°
425°	220°
450°	230°

VOLUME EQUIVALENTS (DRY)

US STANDARD	METRIC (APPROXIMATE)
⅛ TEASPOON	0.5 ML
¼ TEASPOON	1 ML
½ TEASPOON	2 ML
¾ TEASPOON	4 ML
1 TEASPOON	5 ML
1 TABLESPOON	15 ML
¼ CUP	59 ML
⅓ CUP	79 ML
½ CUP	118 ML
⅔ CUP	156 ML
¾ CUP	177 ML
1 CUP	235 ML
2 CUPS OR 1 PINT	475 ML
3 CUPS	700 ML
4 CUPS OR 1 QUART	1 L

WEIGHT EQUIVALENTS

US STANDARD	METRIC (APPROXIMATE)
½ OUNCE	15 G
1 OUNCE	30 G
2 OUNCES	60 G
4 OUNCES	115 G
8 OUNCES	225 G
12 OUNCES	340 G
16 OUNCES OR 1 POUND	455 G

Index

Acknowledgments

Thank you, Samantha, Connor, and John for picking up some of the slack while I worked on this book. Thanks for all the taste testing and help with dishes along the way!

Samantha, thank you for always being by my side in the kitchen when I need you or just for fun. You have the *best* palate and ideas and there is no one on the planet I would rather cook with.

To John and Connor, my favorite recipe testers, who enthusiastically enjoy most of what I create and occasionally join me in the kitchen. Thanks for happily testing things out and for always kissing the cook . . . Now let's work on getting you two in the kitchen more!

Thank you to all the readers of my website, *Souffle Bombay*, and its social media channels. Your comments and feedback make coming up with recipes to share both fun and interesting. I love hearing which recipes are your favorites and how you make them your own.

To my mom, dad, and grandmothers, thanks for being my original inspirations in the kitchen. I love you all!

To America's farmers—and especially dairy farmers—*I see you*. Without you and your passion, dedication, innovation, and 24 hours a day, 7 days a week work ethic, none of us would have access to the bounty of meats, poultry, fruits, and vegetables that we do. Thank you! I try to never take it all for granted.

Thanks to my sister Anita, my niece Skylar, and all my friends and family who like to talk about food. Molly, Maria, Chris, Amy, Patrick, Pete, Eddie, Teddy, Lisa, and many more, I love hearing your ideas, tasting your food, and talking about what we're all making.

To my Inner Food Blogger Circle, thanks for inspiring me, supporting me, teaching me, and putting up with my goofiness. What a crazy job we have!

Thanks to the team at Callisto Media for all your help, patience, and support in the making of this book.

About the Author

Colleen Kennedy is the woman behind the popular food blog *Souffle Bombay* (SouffleBombay.com), where she shares creative recipes that are easy enough for anyone to make to wow their friends and family. She is also the author of *Kid Chef Every Day* and the coauthor of *Picture Me Cooking*. Colleen's work has appeared in various print, online, and television outlets. She has won a number of cooking-related competitions and often goes behind the scenes in the food industry and with America's dairy, beef, and veal farmers, sharing what she learns along the way via her social media channels. You can find Colleen on Instagram, Facebook, Pinterest and Twitter @SouffleBombay.